The **Secretary's Desk Book**

John Harrison

Pitman

PITMAN PUBLISHING LIMITED
128 Long Acre, London WC2E 9AN

A Longman Group Company

© John Harrison 1982

First published in Great Britain 1982
Reprinted 1985

Text set in 10/11 pt Linotron 202 Ehrhardt, printed and bound
in Great Britain at The Bath Press, Avon

ISBN 0 273 01833 7

Contents

Preface

The role of the secretary is changing as a result of the new technologies now being introduced into offices, especially with the emergence of word processing and computerised file-handling facilities. Although the normal practices and procedures for secretarial duties have taken on a new form, the objectives have remained the same with the secretary continuing to provide an efficient communication and administrative service.

The Secretary's Desk Book has been compiled with these objectives in mind by supplying the key factors to practices and procedures and a 'signpost' pointing the way to the acquisition of more detailed up-to-date data. For example, the various references to office machinery and equipment include a representative list of suppliers' names and addresses to enable the secretary to send for details of their very latest products. Indeed the aim throughout the book has been to create an awareness of the procedures and sources for finding any information that may be required.

The Secretary's Desk Book is a practical office guide – an indispensable 'tool' readily available for reference in the desk drawer of the discerning secretary. It is appropriate for all those who are responsible for secretarial services, both those starting out on their careers and those more experienced.

JH 1982

Acknowledgments

I am grateful to the following for permission to reproduce photographs, illustrations and information:

Bell & Howell Ltd
Business Equipment Trade Association
Dictaphone Company Ltd
Flexiform Ltd
Gestetner Ltd
Kodak Ltd
London Regional Transport
Martela Contract Interiors Ltd
3M United Kingdom PLC
Nexos (United Kingdom) Ltd
Office International (GP) Ltd
Pitney Bowes PLC
Project Office Furniture Ltd
St John Ambulance Association
Twinlock PLC

I should also like to express my appreciation to the following people who have contributed in so many different ways to the preparation of this book:

The publishing and production staff of Pitman Publishing Ltd, especially Pam Wickham, Secretarial Studies Publisher, for her expert advice.

My wife for those invaluable secretarial services which she undertook during the preparation of the manuscript.

My colleagues in the Business Studies Department and my secretary, Irene Frankowski, at the Eastleigh College of Further Education, for their valuable criticism and help.

Abbreviations and phrases in common use

AA	Automobile Association
ab initio	from the beginning
ABS	Associate, Chartered Building Societies Institute (FBS – Fellow)
ABTA	Association of British Travel Agents
AC	alternating current
A/c	account
ACA	Associate, Institute of Chartered Accountants (FCA – Fellow)
ACAS	Advisory, Conciliation and Arbitration Service
ACCA	Associate, Association of Certified Accountants (FCCA – Fellow)
ACII	Associate, Chartered Insurance Institute (FCII – Fellow)
ACIPFA	Associate, Chartered Institute of Public Finance Accountants (FCIPFA – Fellow)
ACIS	Associate, Chartered Institute of Secretaries and Administrators (FCIS – Fellow)
ACMA	Associate, Institute of Cost and Management Accountants (FCMA – Fellow)
ADC	advice of duration and charge
ad hoc	for this purpose
ad infinitum	to infinity
ad lib/	
ad libitum	at pleasure
ad val/	
ad valorem	in proportion to the value
AEA	Atomic Energy Authority
AEC	Atomic Energy Commission
AEU	Amalgamated Engineering Union
AFRAeS	Associate Fellow, Royal Aeronautical Society
AFTCom	Associate, Faculty of Teachers in Commerce (FFTCom – Fellow)
AGM	Annual General Meeting
AIA	Associate, Institute of Actuaries (FIA – Fellow)
AIB	Associate, Institute of Bankers (FIB – Fellow)
AIL	Associate, Institute of Linguists (FIL – Fellow)
AIMechE	Associate, Institute of Mechanical Engineers (FIMechE – Fellow; MIMechE – Member)

AInstAM	Associate, Institute of Administrative Management (FInstAM – Fellow; MInstAM – Member)
AInstM	Associate, Institute of Marketing (FInstM – Fellow)
AIOB	Associate, Institute of Builders (FIOB – Fellow)
AIQS	Associate, Institute of Quantity Surveyors (FIQS – Fellow)
ALA	Associate, Library Association (FLA – Fellow)
à la mode	fashionable
AMBIM	Associate Member, British Institute of Management
AMICE	Associate Member, Institute of Civil Engineers (FICE – Fellow)
AMIEE	Associate Member, Institute of Electrical Engineers (FIEE – Fellow)
AMIMechE	Associate Member, Institute of Mechanical Engineers (FIMechE – Fellow)
AMIMunE	Associate Member, Institute of Municipal Engineers (FIMunE – Fellow)
AMIPE	Associate Member, Institute of Production Engineers (FIPE – Fellow)
amp	ampere
AN	advice note
anon	anonymous
AOB	any other business
AP	Associated Press
APEX	Association of Professional, Executive, Clerical and Computer Staffs
AR	all risks (marine insurance)
ARIBA	Associate, Royal Institute of British Architects (FRIBA – Fellow)
ARIC	Associate, Royal Institute of Chemistry (FRIC – Fellow)
ARICS	Associate, Royal Institute of Chartered Surveyors (FRICS – Fellow)
ASCT	Associate, Society of Commercial Teachers (FSCT – Fellow)
ASLEF	Associated Society of Locomotive Engineers and Firemen
ASLIB	Association of Special Libraries and Information Bureaux
AUEW	Amalgamated Union of Engineering Workers
au fait	to be well informed
au revoir	goodbye until we meet again
BA	Bachelor of Arts (MA – Master)/British Airways

BAA	British Airports Authority
BACIE	British Association for Commercial and Industrial Education
BBC	British Broadcasting Corporation
BCh or ChB	Bachelor of Surgery (Mch – Master)
BCom	Bachelor of Commerce (MCom – Master)
BD	Bachelor of Divinity
B/D	bank draft
b/d	brought down
BDA	British Dental Association
B/E	bill of exchange
BEC	Business Education Council
BEd	Bachelor of Education (MEd – Master)
BEM	British Empire Medal
BEng	Bachelor of Engineering (MEng – Master)
BETA	Business Equipment Trades Association
b/f	brought forward
BIM	British Institute of Management
BIR	Board of Inland Revenue
B/L	Bill of lading
BLitt	Bachelor of Letters
BM or MB	Bachelor of Medicine
BMA	British Medical Association
BMTA	British Motor Trades Association
bona fide	of good faith
bon voyage	an expression wishing a traveller a good journey
BOT	Board of Trade
BP	Bill payable
BPhil	Bachelor of Philosophy (MPhil – Master)
BR	British Rail
Br	Bill receivable
B/S	balance sheet/bill of sale
BSA	Building Societies Association
BSc	Bachelor of Science (MSc – Master)
BSC	British Steel Corporation
BSI	British Standards Institution
BST	British summer time
Bt	Baronet
Btu	British thermal unit
BUPA	British United Provident Association
C	Centigrade
c	circa (approx)
©	copyright
C/A	current account
CAA	Civil Aviation Authority
CAP	common agricultural policy (EEC)

carte blanche	full discretionary power; blank paper given to a person on which to write his own terms
CB	Companion of the Bath
CBE	Commander of the Order of the British Empire
CBI	Confederation of British Industry
c/d	carried down
CE	Civil Engineer
CEGB	Central Electricity Generating Board
CEng	Chartered Engineer
CET	Central European Time
cf	compare
c/f	carried forward
CH	Companion of Honour
CID	Criminal Investigation Department/Council of Industrial Design
CIF	cost, insurance and freight
cl	centilitre
cm	centimetre
C/N	credit note
CNAA	Council for National Academic Awards
c/o	care of
COBOL	common business orientated language (computing)
COD	cash on delivery
C of E	Church of England/Council of Europe
COHSE	Confederation of Health Service Employees
COI	Central Office of Information
connoisseur	a critical judge
cordon bleu	first-class cook
Cp	compare
CR	company's risk
Cr	credit/creditor
CRO	Criminal Record Office
CSC	Civil Service Commission
CSU	Civil Service Union
CTT	capital transfer tax
Cum pref	cumulative preference
CVO	Commander of the Royal Victorian Order (MVO – member)
CWO	cash with order
D/A	deposit account
DBE	Dame Commander of the Order of the British Empire
DC	direct current
DCB	Dame Commander of the Most Honourable Order of the Bath
DD	Doctor of Divinity/direct debit

d/d	days after date
deb	debenture
de facto	in fact
DEP	Department of Employment
DES	Department of Education and Science
dft	draft
DHSS	Department of Health and Social Security
div	dividend
DLit	Doctor of Literature
DLitt	Doctor of Letters
DM	Deutschemark
D/N	debit note
DO	delivery order
do.	ditto – the same
DOE	Department of the Environment
DP	data processing
D/P	deferred payment
DPhil	Doctor of Philosophy
Dr	debit/debtor/doctor
DSC/M	Distinguished Service Cross/Medal
DSc	Doctor of Science
DSO	Distinguished Service Order
DTh	Doctor of Theology
DTI	Department of Trade and Industry
DW	dock warrant
E&OE	Errors and omissions excepted
ECGD	Exports Credits Guarantee Department
EDP	electronic data processing
EEC	European Economic Community
EFTA	European Free Trade Association
eg	*exempli gratia* – for example
EMA	European Monetary Agreement
enc	enclosure
en masse	all together
en route	on the way
entente cordiale	friendly understanding
EOC	Equal Opportunities Commission
ERNIE	Electronic random number indicator equipment
ESD	Employment Services Division
ETA	estimated time of arrival
et al.	*et alia* – and others
etc	*et cetera* – and other things
et seq.	*et sequentia* – and the following
ETU	Electrical Trades Union
EURATOM	European Atomic Energy Commission
ex div	exclusive of dividend
ex gratia	as a favour but implying no right

ex officio	by virtue of office
F	fahrenheit
FAI	Fellow, Chartered Auctioneers and Estate Agents Institute
fait accompli	task already completed
faux pas	an error or indiscreet action
FBI	Federation of British Industries
Fo	folio
FOB	free on board
FOQ	free on quay
FOR	free on rail
force majeure	an act of God; excuse for fulfilment of contract
Fortran	formula translation – computing
FTI	*Financial Times* index
FU	follow up
g	gramme
GATT	general agreement on tariffs and trade
GC	George Cross
GCVO	Knight (or Dame) Grand Cross of the Royal Victorian Order
GLC	Greater London Council
GMC	General Medical Council
GMT	Greenwich mean time
GMWU	General and Municipal Workers Union
GP	General Practitioner
GRN	goods received note
ha	hectare
hg	hectogram
hl	hectolitre
hm	hectometre
HMSO	Her Majesty's Stationery Office
Hon	Honorary/Honourable
HP	hire purchase/horse-power
IA	Institute of Actuaries
IATA	International Air Transport Association
IBA	Independent Broadcasting Authority
ib/ibid.	in the same place
id/idem	the same
IDD	International direct dialling
ie/*id est*	that is
IF	insufficient funds (cheques)
II	indorsement irregular (cheques)
ILO	International Labour Organisation
IMF	International Monetary Fund
Inc	incorporated
in extenso	at full length
infra dig	beneath one's dignity

in loc/in loco	in its place
in loco parentis	in the place of a parent
inter alia	among other things
in toto	wholly
intra vires	within the power
inv	invoice
IPS	International paper sizes
ipso facto	by the very fact
IQPS	Institute of Qualified Private Secretaries
IRO	International Refugee Organisation
ISO	International Standards Organisation
ITB	Industrial Training Board
ITU	International Telecommunication Union
J/A	joint account
JP	Justice of the Peace
KBE	Knight Commander of the British Empire
KCB	Knight Commander of the Most Honourable Order of the Bath
KG	Knight of the Order of the Garter
kg	kilogram
kl	kilolitre
km	kilometre
kw	kilowatt
l	litre
L/C	letter of credit/lower case
LCCI	London Chamber of Commerce and Industry
LlB	Bachelor of Laws
LlD	Doctor of Laws
lm	lumen
locum tenens	a deputy
LS	*locus sigilli* – the place of the seal
Ltd	Limited
LV	luncheon voucher
m	metre
M	Monsieur
MA	Master of Arts
MAAT	Member, Association of Accounting Technicians
MB	Bachelor of Medicine
MBE	Member of the Order of the British Empire
MC	Military Cross
MD	Doctor of Medicine
mg	milligram
Mgr	Monsignor/Monseigneur
MIAE	Member, Institution of Automobile Engineers
MICE	Member, Institution of Civil Engineers
MICR	magnetic ink character recognition

MIChemE	Member, Institution of Chemical Engineers
MIEE	Member, Institution of Electrical Engineers
MIMechE	Member, Institution of Mechanical Engineers
MInstPS	Member, Institute of Purchasing and Supply
MIPM	Member, Institute of Personnel Management (FIPM – Fellow)
ml	millilitre
MLA	Member, Legislative Assembly
MLC	Member, Legislative Council
Mlle	Mademoiselle
MLR	minimum lending rate
mm	millimetre
MO	money order
modus operandi	method of working
MP	Member of Parliament
MS	manuscript
MSC	Manpower Services Commission
MSS	manuscripts
MTh	Master of Theology
NALGO	National Association of Local Government Officers
NAS	National Association of School Masters
NATFHE	National Association of Teachers in Further and Higher Education
NATO	North Atlantic Treaty Organisation
NATSOPA	National Society of Operative Printers and Assistants
NB	*nota bene* – note thoroughly
NCB	National Coal Board
NCCL	National Council for Civil Liberties
NCR	no carbon required
NEB	National Enterprise Board
NEDC	National Economic Development Council
nem con	*nemine contradicente* – no one contradicting
NFU	National Farmers Union
NHS	National Health Service
NI	National insurance
No	number
NOP	National opinion poll
NP	Notary Public
N/P	net proceeds
NR	no risk (insurance)
NRDC	National Research Development Corporation
NTDA	National Trade Development Association
NUGMW	National Union of General and Municipal Workers
NUJ	National Union of Journalists
NUM	National Union of Mineworkers

NUPE	National Union of Public Employees
NUR	National Union of Railwaymen
NUS	National Union of Students
NUT	National Union of Teachers
O & M	Organisation and Methods
OBE	Order of the British Empire
O/D	overdraft
OECD	Organisation for Economic Co-operation and Development
OFT	Office of Fair Trading
OHMS	On Her Majesty's Service
OM	Order of Merit
OPEC	Organisation of Petroleum Exporting Countries
OR	owner's risk
OS	Ordnance Survey
p	page
pa	per annum
PA	Press Association
PABX	private automatic branch exchange
P & P	postage and packing
PAYE	pay as you earn
PC	Privy Councillor/petty cash/police constable
PEI	Pitmans Examinations Institute
per capita	each per unit
per cent	*per centum* – for every hundred
per se	by itself
PhD	Doctor of Philosophy
P/L	profit and loss
PLA	Port of London Authority
PLC	Public limited company
PM	Prime Minister
PMBX	private manual branch exchange
PN	promissory note
PO	postal order/post office
POP	post office preferred (envelope)
post mortem	after death
pp	pages/per pro (on behalf of)
prima facie	on the face of it
pro forma	as a matter of form
pro rata	in proportion
pro tem	*pro tempore* – for the time being
PSDip	Private Secretary's Diploma
QC	Queen's Counsel
quasi	similar to
quid pro quo	something for something
qv	*quod vide* – which see

RAC	Royal Automobile Club
R/D	refer to drawer (cheques)
Re	with reference to
RIBA	Royal Institute of British Architects
RICS	Royal Institute of Chartered Surveyors
rm	ream
RP	reply paid
RPI	retail price index
RSA	Royal Society of Arts
RSVP	*répondez s'il vous plait* – please reply
SAE	stamped, addressed envelope
SALT	Strategic Arms Limitation Treaty
SAV	stock at valuation
SAYE	save as you earn
SCOTBEC	Scottish Business Education Council
SE	Stock Exchange
seq	*sequentes* – the following
SHAPE	Supreme Headquarters of the Allied Powers in Europe
sine die	without an appointed day
S/N	shipping note
SO	standing order
Soc	Society
SOGAT	Society of Graphical and Allied Trades
SOR	sale or return
status quo	no change
STD	subscriber trunk dialling
stet	let it stand
stg.	sterling
sub judice	under judicial consideration
t	tonne
TB	trial balance
TEC	Technician Education Council
TGWU	Transport and General Workers Union
TM	trade mark
TOPS	training opportunities scheme
TSD	Training Services Division
TUC	Trades Union Congress
UDI	unilateral declaration of independence
ultra vires	beyond legal authority
UNESCO	United Nations Educational, Scientific and Cultural Organisation
UNO	United Nations Organisation
UPU	Universal Postal Union
USDAW	Union of Shop, Distributive and Allied Workers
VAT	value added tax

VC	Victoria Cross
VDU	visual display unit
verbatim	word for word
vice versa	the other way round
VIP	very important person
viva voce	by word of mouth
viz	*videlicet* – namely
w	watt
WEA	Workers Educational Association
wef	with effect from
WHO	World Health Organisation
WMO	World Meteorological Organisation
WP	word processing/without prejudice

Addressing envelopes

```
For the attention of Mr P Stringer

Messrs Johnson, Williams & Sons
120 Old Steine
BRIGHTON
Sussex
BN2 4DU
```

Example of an addressed envelope

1 Type the address parallel with the long side of the envelope.
2 Centre the addressee's name and start it half-way down the
   envelope to allow sufficient space for the postage stamps and
   postmarks.
3 Begin each item of the address on a separate line and use
   single spacing. The block method is normally preferred.
4 Use block capitals for the post town.
5 Use block capitals for the postcode and place it at the bottom
   of the address.

6   Normally include the name of the county. A list of post towns not requiring county names is given in the *Post Office Guide*.

7   Place any special directions, such as 'Private', 'Confidential' or 'For the attention of . . . ' clear of the address – usually a double space above the name.

8   Use titles as follows:

Mrs or Ms – for a married lady
It is usual to use her husband's christian name or initial.
Examples: Mrs J R Barnes, Ms W Harris

Miss or Ms – for a single lady
Examples: Miss R A Smart, Ms P Finch
NB: Ms is used when a lady indicates that she prefers to use this title in preference to a title indicating her marital status.

The Misses – for unmarried sisters
Example: The Misses P & L Spencer

Mr or Esq – for a man
Mr is normally preferred.
Example: Mr J Partridge

Mr & Mrs – for husband and wife using the husband's christian name or initials
Example: Mr & Mrs George Smith

Messrs – for a partnership
Example: Messrs Stanley & Jackson
NB: 'Messrs' should not be used before the name of a limited company, eg Pitman Books Limited.

Reference sources:
Post Office Guide   – for advice on addressing envelopes
Postcode directories   – for postcodes
Telephone directories – for postal towns

Types and sizes of envelopes: see Stationery p 132
Addressing machines : see Office equipment p 97

Advertising

1   Selecting the newspaper or journal:
   • choose those which will be read by the people the advertisement aims to reach
   • refer to *Willing's Press Guide* or *Newspaper Press Directory* for details of names, addresses and telephone numbers of newspapers and journals and their publication days

Example of an advertisement

2   When drafting the advertisement:
- use words sparingly, selecting only those which will attract the attention of readers and give the salient facts
- create interest by including information which will encourage readers to respond to the advertisement, eg when advertising a vacancy, state the salary offered
- state clearly any basic requirements, eg shorthand speed of 100 wpm, so that only those qualified will apply
- display the draft in a suitable style and in the manner required for publication, giving prominence to any eye-catching information

3   When submitting the advertisement to the newspaper or journal state:
- the type of advertisement required, ie classified or display
- the amount of space you require
- the date when you require the advertisement to be published

Appointments

When making appointments for your employer:

1   Be conscious of the routine office matters with which the employer prefers to deal at specific times of the day.

2   Enter appointments in both your employer's diary and your own. Provisional appointments should be entered in pencil first and inked in when they are confirmed.

3   Confirm by letter any appointment made by telephone.

4 Allow sufficient travelling time between appointments arranged outside the office on the same day.
5 Meetings can extend beyond their estimated finishing time and care should be taken when arranging appointments which follow them.
6 If a caller requests an appointment and a date and time are agreed, make a note of the caller's name, address and telephone number in case you need to contact them to amend the date or time.
7 If you are in doubt about an appointment, possibly because it is requested at a time which is after hours or involves the employer's wife, make it a provisional one and consult your employer as soon as possible. When it is agreed with the employer write a letter of confirmation to the person concerned.

Bank services

Deposit account – giving interest on money invested
Current account – using cheques and cheque cards to make payments
Personal budget account – spreading the outlay on expenditure
Lending to approved borrowers – acquiring bank loan/overdraft
Standing orders, direct debits – making regular payments through the bank
Credit transfer, credit cards – transferring credit from one account to another
Cash cards – withdrawing cash from cash dispensers at the bank
Drafts, bills of exchange, letters of credit, mail and telegraphic transfer, computer message switching system, foreign currency, travellers cheques – making payments abroad
Night safe – depositing money after bank hours
Safe keeping – depositing securities, jewellery etc
Business/professional services – using services such as: executor, trustee, investment management, insurance advice, finance of exports/imports

The banks supply leaflets giving further information on all aspects of banking.

Current account

Advice for bank current account holders:

1   Keep your cheque book in a safe place. If it is lost or stolen, advise the bank and the police immediately. It is advisable to keep a separate record of your account number.
2   When making out a cheque:
    - always use a pen
    - write the payee's name exactly as described in the invoice or notice to pay, eg J R Brooks & Sons
    - write the amount of pounds in words as well as in figures
    - begin writing as far to the left as possible and do not leave spaces for other words or figures to be added; draw a line to close up all blank spaces
    - the date must contain the day, month and year
    - sign the cheque with your normal signature as supplied to the bank
    - cross the cheque if it has to be sent through the post
    - keep a record of the date, payee's name and amount on the counterfoil
3   If you have a cheque card keep it separately from your cheque book for security reasons.
4   When transferring amounts from your account to another bank account you will need to quote your bank, branch and account numbers. On other occasions you may need to refer to the cheque serial number. These numbers are located on cheques, as follows:
    a   Bank and branch number eg 40–09–18
    b   Account number eg 12345678
    c   Cheque serial number eg 460423
5   When paying money into a bank account check the following points:
    - cheques bear current dates
    - amounts in words and figures are the same
    - payee's names are correct
    - cheques are signed
    - any alterations on cheques are clear and have been signed
    - cross any open cheques
6   Complete a paying-in slip with the following details:
    Date
    Bank code no, name and branch
    Name* and account no of payee
    Cash (notes and coins)*
    Cheques (listed separately)*; state total number
    Signature of person paying-in
7   Bank statements, issued by the bank, should be kept safely in

---

* also entered on counterfoil

a wallet. A statement is a copy of the customer's account with the bank and it shows:

- balance of the account at the end of the previous statement
- credits for money paid into the account
- debits for money paid out by cheques and other means
- debits for bank charges
- balance of the account at the end of this statement

The entries should be checked and any new items, such as charges, should be recorded.

Overseas travel facilities

Overseas travel facilites provided by banks

Services for people travelling abroad:

Travellers cheques It is advisable to use travellers cheques for most of the money to be taken abroad as they can be cashed in most banks and are normally accepted in hotels, restaurants, airports and shops in place of cash. They can be supplied in a wide range of currencies, such as sterling; French and Swiss francs; US, Canadian, Australian and Hong Kong dollars; Japanese yen, etc, and are as acceptable as cash to the local trades people if they are made out in the currency of the country being visited. Since they are used as cash it is wise to arrange with the bank to have a mixture of small and large denominations to cater for different amounts. A bank will usually require several days' notice to supply travellers cheques and before they will release the cheques they have to be signed at the bank by the person travelling.

Foreign bank notes Whilst most money taken abroad should be in travellers cheques it is useful to have some foreign money for use immediately on arrival for such things as taxi fares, postage stamps, refreshments, etc. The bank normally requires a few days' notice to supply foreign bank notes. There are restrictions on the amount of currency that you can take in or out of some countries but the bank will give you advice on this. When returning from abroad it is advisable to change as many coins as possible into notes as the banks do not usually exchange coins of low value. Moreover, the exchange rates for large amounts of coins are less favourable than for notes. NB: The *Notice to travellers* leaflet supplied by banks and travel agents is a useful source of information concerning currency regulations and exchange.

Cheque cards It is possible for ordinary cheques to be cashed (up to the value of £50 each) at banks abroad which display the Eurocheque symbol.

Credit cards Credit cards, such as Barclay, Access or American Express may also be used abroad to pay for goods and services on credit from traders participating in these credit card schemes. Credit cards can also be used for obtaining cash from certain banks abroad.

Insurance A bank can arrange travel insurance to include protection of baggage, medical and personal accident cover and compensation for the cancellation of travel arrangements.

Passports Forms for obtaining passports can be obtained from a bank.

See also Travel arrangements p 143

British Standards Specifications

British Standards Specifications are obtainable from the British Standards Institution, British Standards House, 2 Park Street, London W1A 2BS, or they may be referred to in principal public libraries. The following is a selection of the specifications which are of interest to secretaries:

Dictation equipment	3738:	1980
Duplicators and copiers	5479:	1977

Envelopes – terms and sizes		4264: 1976
Filing – dimensions of folders and files		1467: 1972
Forms – letterheads and continuous stationery		1808: 1967/1970

Business documents

Document	Prepared by	Distribution
Stores requisition	Person in department requesting goods from stock – countersigned by head of department	Storekeeper
Purchases requisition	Person in department requesting goods to be purchased – countersigned by head of department	Storekeeper/ buyer
Price list	Sales department	Customers
Quotation	Sales department	Customers
Order	Buyer	Supplier Stores Accounts Buyer
Advice note	Despatch	Customer
Delivery note	Despatch	Driver Customer
Goods received note	Stores	Accounts Buyer
Invoice	Sales	Customer Accounts Despatch Sales Stores
Credit note	Sales	Customer Accounts Despatch Sales Stores
Statement	Accounts	Customer Accounts

Office furniture – desks and chairs	5940:	1980
Printers' correction signs	5261:	1975/1976
Typewriters	2481:	1975
Typewriting terms	4268:	1980

Purpose

A request to the storekeeper to issue stock

A request to the storekeeper/buyer to order goods

To provide customers with a brief description and
current prices of goods offered for sale
To provide customers with full particulars of goods or
services offered for sale and the conditions of sale.
Similar information may be supplied in an estimate
A request to the seller to supply goods

Informs customer that the order has been despatched
or is ready for despatch
Serves as an advice of goods delivered (for customer)
and a receipt for goods delivered (for supplier)
Internal document notifying accounts, stores and buyer
of the arrival of goods and their condition
Informs customer of goods purchased and the amounts
charged

Notifies customer of a reduction in the amount charged
on an invoice

A record of transactions for a given period informing
the customer of the total amount owing and requesting
payment

Suppliers of office forms and stationery

BPC Business Forms PLC, Whitehall Road, Leeds LS12 1BD
The Copeland Chatterson Co Ltd, Seymour House, 17 Waterloo Place, London SW1Y 4AR
Kalamazoo Ltd, Northfield, Birmingham B31 2RW
Kenrick & Jefferson Ltd, High Street, West Bromwich, West Midlands B70 8NB
Moore Paragon UK Ltd, Moore House, 75–79 Southwark Street, London SE1 0HY
Snows Business Forms Ltd, Third Avenue, Millbrook, Southampton

Carbon copying

Carbons are supplied in different grades, colours, weights and sizes:

Carbon paper weights	*No of copies*
Super heavyweight	1–2
Heavyweight	1–3
Standard weight	4–6
Manifold (lightweight)	7–10
Super manifold (lightweight)	11–15

Colours: black, blue, purple, green, red, brown

To increase number of carbon copies obtained from one master, remember:

- Weight and quality of carbon paper ⎫
- Weight of the copy paper ⎭ – thinner paper reproduces more copies
- Strength of the platen – a hard platen is best for reproducing many copies
- Condition of the carbon paper – new paper will reproduce more copies than used paper
- Setting of the pressure control on the typewriter
- Typewriter used – an electric typewriter reproduces more copies than a manual typewriter
- Condition of the typeface – a clean typeface is essential to obtain distinct impressions

Types of carbon paper

Standard carbon paper (in general use) Carbons are frequently made with a special plastic coating on the back which prevents them from curling.

Plastic film ('long-life' carbons) These use a microporous plastic coating impregnated with a quick-drying ink. After the typewriter key strikes the film, transferring ink to the copy paper, further supplies of ink replace that used. This allows the film to be re-used about 200 times to produce quality copies.

One-time carbon paper This paper, which is supplied and fixed in position by the manufacturer, is intended for use once only. It is normally used for stencils and invoice sets.

Carbon backed forms These forms have a carbon coating which takes the place of separate sheets of carbon paper.

Care of carbon paper

1 Keep the carbon paper in a flat box.
2 Store the carbon paper box in a cool place – away from a heater or the sun.
3 Periodically turn the carbon paper upside down in order to use it evenly.
4 Be especially careful when fitting the copy paper and carbon paper into the typewriter, as careless handling creases the paper. If the papers feed unevenly, ask a mechanic to check whether the feed roll mechanism requires adjustment.

Alternatives to carbon paper:

Reproducing copies on an office copier This practice is becoming more popular with the increased use of copiers.

NCR (no carbon required) The reverse side of the top copy and the top sides of the sheets below are specially treated with chemical to reproduce copies without the need for carbon paper.

Carbon-free copying paper The top copy has an emulsion coating of dye on the back and the top side of the second sheet is coated with a clay material. When pressure is applied to the top sheet, the coating of dye penetrates the clay surface of the second sheet and a blue copy is made. When more than one copy is required, intermediate sheets are inserted which have the clay coating on the top and the dye coating at the back.

Correction of errors: see p 31.

Circulation of documents

Different methods of circulating documents within an organisation:

1 Type **carbon copies** with the names of the recipients included in a list at the bottom of the first page. A tick is placed against the name to whom each individual copy is sent, eg:

cc

Sales Manager
Chief Buyer
Chief Accountant ✓
Personnel Manager
Works Manager

2 As above, but instead of typing carbon copies, they are **reproduced** on an office copier or word processor. It is, however, necessary to write or type the distribution list on the original before it is copied.

3 Distribute the original document(s) with a **circulation slip** attached. Each recipient would be requested to take the necessary action, delete their name from the list and pass on the document(s) to the next person on the list.

4 Use a **computer linked by VDUs**.

5 Use **facsimile telegraphy** for distribution of documents between branches of a firm.

6 Distribute the original document(s) in an **internal mail envelope**.

Communications in business

The different forms of business communication are listed below. For fuller information, turn to the pages indicated.

Cable – urgent written communication abroad
Ceefax – BBC televised information service (p 142)
Computer terminal – transmitting and receiving computer data (p 28)

Confravision – Post Office service for closed circuit television of conferences (p 141)

Dictating machine – communicating to typist (pp 101–4)

Face-to-face conversation – ideal for personal/confidential matters

Facsimile telegraphy – enables replicas of documents to be sent any distance with complete accuracy – combines the speed of the telephone with the reproduction facility of the office copier (p 140)

Intercom – internal oral communication

Letter – written communication of any length (pp 34–8)

Loudspeaker – public address system – conveys information to a large number of people

Memo – written communication within an organisation (p 38)

Meeting – useful for collecting the views of several people, the information being conveyed by minutes or reports (pp 85–91)

Micropad – handwritten input to computer

Microwriter – keying-in, recording and printing data

Notice board – displaying information for a large number of people

Oracle – ITV televised information service (p 142)

Paging – location of staff as they move around a building

Prestel – Post Office televised information service (p 142)

Radio – oral communication from one motor vehicle to another

Report – written information for several people (p 125)

Telegram / telemessage – urgent written information at home and abroad (p 139)

Telephone – internal and external oral communication (pp 135–9)

Telephone answering machine – recording telephone messages (p 138)

Teleprinter/telex – combines the speed of the telephone with the authority of the written word (pp 139–40)

Telex pad – handwritten input for sending telex messages

Television – closed circuit – sending data within an organisation

Word processor – after processing, information is printed or communicated by telephone direct to a correspondent (p 109)

Factors to be considered when choosing a method of communication:

- Speed of delivery   – telephone an urgent message
- Reliability   – written communication, such as letters or telex, ensure accuracy

• Security	– registered letter for valuables
• Destination – internal	– memo or intercom
external: in this country	– letter or telex
external: abroad	– airmail letter or telex
• Length of communication	– short: memo or telephone
	– long: letter or report
• Written or oral	– written communication, such as telex, if a permanent record is required, otherwise a telephone message will do
• Cost of transmitting the message	– telephone is cheap for local calls, but not for an overseas correspondent
• Influence	– face-to-face conversation is usually more effective than a written message
• Equipment at the disposal of the recipient	– telex or facsimile telegraphy
• Number of people to receive the communication	– notice board or meeting for a large number
• Appearance of the message	– greetings telemessage for a special occasion

Computing and word processing glossary of terms

Access time Time taken to find and read data from a memory device.

Address Reference number or name which identifies a particular area of computer storage.

ADP Automatic data processing.

ALGOL Algorithmic language, ie a high-level programming language used for scientific applications.

Alphanumeric A combination of alphabetical letters, numerical digits and sometimes special characters which can be processed by computer.

Assembler A program for translating an assembly code into a machine code.

Backing store Computer storage such as magnetic discs and tapes used to supplement the main store.

Basic An acronym for 'beginner's all-purpose symbolic instruction code' – a programming language used mainly with micro-computers and time-sharing systems.

Batch Quantity of records or data which form a unit of work for processing by computer.

Batch processing A process of coding and collating items into groups before processing.

Binary code Arithmetical process of counting in twos.

Bit Contracted from *bi*nary dig*it* representing a zero or one in binary arithmetic.

Boiler plating Using a selected group of standard paragraphs and merging them to form one document.

Bug An error in a program or computer system.

Byte 8 bits = 1 byte – a byte representing one alphabetical or numerical symbol.

Central processor (or CPU) Central part of a computer system containing the control unit, main store and arithmetic/logic unit; controls the operations of the computer, interpreting and executing instructions.

Character string Group of identical alphabetic/numeric characters, eg words, date, etc, appearing within a text; a search can be made by comparing a character string with the characters contained in a document.

Chip Integrated electronic circuit created on a silicon wafer to perform complex automated operations.

COBOL – 'Common business orientated language', a high-level programming language used for data processing.

COM Acronym for 'computer output on microfilm' or 'computer originated microfilm': a process used for preparing microfilm directly from a computer.

Command key Used in a word processing system to activate an operator command.

Compiler A program which converts high-level language to low-level machine language.

Constant Data which remains unchanged during a complete process.

Control key Operated simultaneously with another key to provide access to editing or formating for setting margins, inserting spaces, etc.

Cursor Device on a video screen for positioning the next entry.

Daisy-wheel Printing element used in conjunction with a printer in a word processor.

Data Information which has been coded for processing.

Data base A set of related files providing a data processing base which can be used by several programs.

Data capture Method of recording information before processing.

Data preparation Converting data into a form which can be read automatically by machine.

Data processing Ordering and sorting data to produce the desired results.

Data transmission Movement of data from one device (computer, word processor, etc) to another by means of a communication network.

Direct (or random) access Access of data in any order; data does not have to be sorted since access is made directly to the master record required; only those records which need changing have to be accessed.

Disk/disc Flat metal disc coated with a magnetic material for storing text or programs.

Diskette (see floppy disc).

Dot matrix printer Output device on a computer or word processor which uses a dot matrix for printing.

EDP 'Electronic data processing'.

Emboldening Overprinting to reproduce bolder type.

Erase Removing data from storage without replacing it.

Field Subdivision of an item of information, eg a customer's account number.

File Single unit of related records used in a computer system.

Floppy disc (or diskette) Flexible magnetic disc for storage and rapid access of data used mainly in mini-computers, micro-computers and word processors.

Flow chart Diagram using special symbols to depict the various stages in a system or computer program.

Format Layout and design of a document.

Fortran Acronym for 'formula translator', a high-level programming language used for mathematical and scientific computations.

Function key Used to activate an operation or format command.

Global search and replace Searching for a character string and replacing it with a different one, eg changing all references to 1982 to 1983.

Hard copy Machine output in readable printed form.

Hardware Physical parts of a computer system, including the computer itself and peripherals such as printers and terminals.

High-level language Programming language designed to simplify the writing of complex programs without having to use machine language.

IDP Integrated data processing, in which the same files are used by different programs.

Immediate access (or core) store A short-term memory of the central processing unit used for holding data to be processed.

Inkjet printer High-speed printer which electrostatically charges ink on to paper to produce a high-quality image.

Input The process of feeding data into a computer.

Input device Converts information into a form which can be stored in a computer memory.

Interface Link between a word processor and a peripheral such as a disc drive.

Kilobyte 1000 bytes or characters.

Line printer Prints the results from a computer one line at a time.

Machine code/language Low-level basic language used in computer programming.

Magnetic card, magnetic disk Data storage devices.

Mainframe Another term for a central processing unit.

Mark sense reading Automatic reading of marks recorded on documents for input to a computer.

Megabyte 1000000 bytes or characters.

Memory Computer device for storing information.

Menu Method of making a word processing system 'user friendly': sets of commands are displayed on the screen so that the operator does not have to constantly refer to a manual.

Merge Combining text from two separate files.

MICR 'Magnetic ink character recognition': printing magnetic ink numbers on the bottom of cheques for automatic reading and sorting, eg

⑈⑈·⑈000651⑈⑈·⑈ 00⑈⑈·⑈0000⑈: ⑈0476375⑈⑈·⑈ ⑈⑈

Microprocessor Small processor which controls the operation of a computer or word processor.

Mode Operating function such as insert, delete or merge on a word processor.

Modem Acronym for 'modulator–demodulator'; used to convert computer input/output into a form which can be sent by telephone.

Multi-access System in which several users have access to one processor at the same time.

OCR 'Optical character recognition', an input process using alphanumeric characters, usually in pencil, which can be read by a scanning device; see also MICR.

Off-line Part of a data processing system but not directly connected to a computer.

OMR 'Optical mark recognition', an input process in which lines are printed within a pre-determined area to be read by a scanning device, as in the following example:

On-line A terminal interacting directly with a computer.

Output Information transferred from the computer's memory unit to a storage or output device.

Peripheral Any part of a computer system which is linked to the central processor, eg disk drive, printer etc.

Program Sequence of instructions to a computer to perform particular tasks.

PROM 'Programmable read-only memory'.

Prompt Instructions which help the operator of a word processor to carry out the correct procedure or identify faulty actions.

RAM 'Random access memory', temporary storage where each item can be read or updated at the same time, irrespective of its location.

Random access See Direct access.

Real time Processing data where each transaction is fully processed at the time of operation, as in an airline seat reservation system.

Retrieval Extraction of information from a computer file.

ROM 'Read only memory', permanent storage which cannot be updated.

Scrolling Moving text vertically or horizontally on a screen.

Search and replace Searching for characters and replacing them by different ones.

Serial (or sequential) access Locating information by searching for it in order or sequence in which it is stored.

Shared logic system Computer or word processing system in which several terminals have access to the same central processor, storage devices and printer.

Silicon chip See Chip.

Software Non-physical parts of a computer system, ie the programs and operating manuals.

Stand-alone system Single computer or word processor standing alone without any terminals connected.

Status line Appears at the top or bottom of a word processor screen giving information about the work situation under review, eg name of file, column line, page number etc.

Store See Memory.

Terminal Peripheral device (usually a keyboard with a printer and/or visual display unit) for feeding information into a computer (input) and extracting information from a computer (output).

Time sharing Several users having simultaneous access to the computer facilities.

Update Changes in a master file brought about by the insertion of current information.

VDU 'Visual display unit', a peripheral device which displays data on a screen.

Word processor Electronic equipment used for preparing text, including editing, storage, retrieval and transmission of information; see also p 109.

Word-wraparound Automatically transferring the last word(s) on a line to the next line if it does not fit within the line length.

Conference planning

1 Before any arrangements can be made, decisions must be taken by the employer or conference organising committee concerning:
   a theme or purpose of the conference
   b date
   c place
   A new file should be opened for each conference and all documents relevant to the conference should be kept in it.

2 Select the conference venue and hotels suitable for accommodating the delegates. You will need to consider the rooms and conference facilities available; cost and accessibility by road and rail.

3 Arrange a meeting with the employer or conference organising committee to discuss the programme. Include suggestions for chairmen, speakers, social activities, mayor's or company chairman's reception (if appropriate).

4 Write to the chairmen and speakers for each session, inviting them to take part. Make arrangements for the social activities and reception.

5 A preliminary notice of the conference should be circulated to delegates, and possibly a notice in a professional journal.

6 Discuss the programme with the conference hotel/centre and make the arrangements for rooms, catering etc.

7 Make arrangements for the printing and despatch of the conference programme, booking form (giving details of recommended hotels) and invitation cards for the social events. At this stage the charges for delegates can be calculated and included in the programme. If it is a company conference, charges will be met by the company.

8   If there is to be a conference dinner, the following arrangements may be necessary:
    a invite special guests and arrange for the after-dinner speeches
    b arrange entertainment
    c arrange for cocktails in an ante-room for guests
    d discuss the menu, wines and floral decorations with the hotel
    e book a photographer
    f arrange for the printing of the menu card
    g draw up a table plan with place names

9   Book a room at the conference centre to serve as a conference office to deal with registration of delegates, preparation and issue of conference papers and to supply information to delegates. Arrange a rota of staff to work in the conference office for the duration of the conference.

10 Arrange for the recording of the conference proceedings and, if appropriate, for the press to be invited to the public sessions.

11 Arrange for visual aids to be available for speakers and check on the provision of amplifying equipment.

12 Arrange for the secure transportation and insurance against loss, theft, etc of any items of value to be used at the conference and make a record of the serial numbers of all items of equipment transported.

13 Arrange with the AA or RAC for direction signs to be installed in the town.

14 When the booking forms and cheques arrive, make arrangements with the bank to open a special conference account and pay the cheques into it. Acknowledge the booking forms and cheques. Keep a careful check on the number of bookings received so that you do not accept more people than can be accommodated.

15 At a date to be agreed, confirm the number of bookings with the conference centre and hotels concerned.

16 After the conference:
    a write letters of thanks to the chairmen, speakers and all who contributed to the conference
    b arrange for the payment of speakers, entertainments, florist, hotels, etc
    c prepare a report of the conference for issue to delegates and possibly for the press
    d despatch conference photographs to delegates
    e prepare a receipts and payments account for the accountant or for submission to the next meeting of the conference organising committee
    f any problems encountered at the conference should be noted in the conference file so that these can be avoided when planning future functions of a similar nature.

Correction of errors – hints for typists

Typescript

	Rubber	Correction fluid	Correction paper	Correction ribbon
Check typing thoroughly and correct any errors before removing the paper from the typewriter	√	√	√	√
Use the eraser to remove the error completely	√	√	√	√
Type in the correction to provide an exact match with the other typing	√	√	√	√
Be careful not to dirty the paper with finger marks when making an erasure	√	√	√	√
If the paper has been removed from the typewriter before the correction has been made: Replace the paper and align the existing type by using the paper-release lever and variable-line spacer. Note that the typing line should be level with the line indicator	√	√	√	√
When erasing, move the carriage, using margin-release key, to the extreme right or left-hand position	√	√		
Apply the fluid evenly over the error, without using an excessive amount, otherwise when it is dry a mound will appear above the paper surface and the correction will be indistinct. Wait until the fluid is completely dry before typing correction		√		
The pencil-type eraser can be sharpened with a pencil sharpener to give a pointed end. This makes it easier to	√			

	Rubber	Correction fluid	Correction paper	Correction ribbon
erase a single character without removing any unnecessary typing				
When using correction paper be careful not to use the same place more than once, otherwise it will not remove the whole of the error.			✓	
A correction ribbon is an integral part of an electric 'self-correcting' typewriter and is a very efficient and quick method of correcting errors. The error is removed by using the back spacer, typing the incorrect character with the corrrection ribbon engaged and then typing the correct character with the normal ribbon				✓

Carbon copies

1 Place a small piece of paper behind each sheet of carbon, in the position where the erasure is to be made.
2 Erase the top copy.
3 Lift the first sheet of carbon, erase the error on the copy and remove the piece of paper.
4 Proceed as before for the additional copies.
5 Before typing in the correct word or letter, make sure that all the temporary pieces of paper have been removed.

Ink stencils

Hold the stencil clear of the carbon and paint over the error with a correcting fluid. Allow the fluid to dry and then type in the correct characters, leaving no trace of the error.

Spirit masters

It is necessary to remove the carbon impression on the glossy side of the master. The following methods may be used:
1 A soft eraser (made specially for the purpose) will absorb the dye and, at the same time, replace the original surface of the master paper. Although it leaves a dirty mark, this will not show up on the copies.
2 A correcting fluid may be painted very thinly over the error to replace the clear china clay backing.

3   A sharp instrument may be used to scrape away the dye, but the disadvantage with this method is that it may also scrape away the china clay backing on the master.

To make the correction, insert a piece of unused transfer sheet behind the master, so that the dye content of the alteration will be the same as for the rest of the master. Type in the correction using the same pressure as for the original typing.

Offset litho masters

Offset litho masters are normally prepared on a plate-maker from an original typed on bond paper. Any errors made when typing would be corrected by one of the methods listed under Typescript (p 31), although the fluid is generally considered to be the most effective. If direct-image plates are used, an offset eraser should be used for making corrections. Medium pressure should be applied to remove the greasy part of the image, leaving only a faint 'ghost' image. Try to avoid scraping the surface of the plate, since this will damage the coating and prevent the correction from appearing clearly. The correct characters should be retyped using exactly the same pressure as before when using a fabric ribbon, but on typewriters fitted with paper or acetate ribbons it may be necessary to give each character a double stroke to make a correction. An alternative method of correcting a paper plate is by using a specially-prepared 'grease-free' erasing fluid.

Word processing

Procedures for the correction of errors vary with the different word processing systems, but the following methods are commonly used:

- To amend a character or word discovered whilst typing the line
  - back-space to the error (this automatically erases all characters up to that point) and re-type the correct material

- To amend a single character after completion of a paragraph or page
  - position cursor under the incorrect character and key in the correct one

- To delete character(s), words or paragraphs
  - position cursor under the unwanted character(s) and press the delete key: the text is automatically adjusted to correct the spacing

- To add character(s)
  - position cursor under the character following the omission, press the insert key and key in the new

	character: the text is automatically adjusted in length to accommodate the new material
• To amend a group of identical characters in a text, ie a character string	– carry out the procedure for global search and replace

Correspondence: key factors in composition and construction

1 **Date** It is essential to date all correspondence – state the day, month and year, eg 14 January 19—.
2 **Reference** To give a letter a means of identification, state your reference and that of the addressee if one is provided.
3 **Telephone extension** When letters are sent from large organisations, it is helpful if the writer's telephone extension number is inserted in the heading.
4 **Inside name and address** This is the name and address of the addressee and should be accommodated in three or four lines, if possible. When the letter is being despatched in a window envelope, the postal town should be in capitals followed by the post code.
5 **Security notations** If these are required, they are shown above the inside name and address for the following reasons:

Personal or Private	– to indicate that the letter should be opened and read only by the addressee
Confidential	– to indicate that the letter should be opened and read only by the addressee or by those he has authorised to do so.
Personal & Confidential or Private & Confidential	– as in Personal or Private above

6 **Attention line** If the letter has to be addressed to an

organisation but you know the name of the person who will deal with it, it is helpful to include an attention line above the inside name and address, eg For the attention of Mrs J Hicks.

7 **Heading** Use one if possible as it is a quick reference to the content of the document. A letter in reply to one with a heading should be given the same subject heading.

8 **Salutation and complimentary close** These are normally either:

    formal   – Dear Sir
                Yours faithfully
    informal – Dear Mr Smith or Dear John
                Yours sincerely

9 **Paragraphing** Divide the letter into paragraphs, each dealing with one point only and arranged as follows:

    a introductory paragraph
    b body of the letter (further subdivided into paragraphs)
    c concluding paragraph

The message in a long letter is easier to follow and understand when the different points are made in small paragraphs, arranged in a logical order with each point leading logically to the next.

10 **Introductory paragraph** This should follow on from the heading and introduce the subject matter by referring to any previous letter, telephone conversation or, if there has been no previous correspondence, directly to the subject matter.

11 **Concluding paragraph** This will normally indicate to the addressee the next stage in the communication as the writer sees it.

12 **Signature block** This should contain the name of the writer and his title/description, eg:

    a when employer dictates   – Yours faithfully
        a letter and signs it   BETA DYNAMICS PLC
                        (*signature*)
                        John Smith
                        Marketing Manager

    b when employer dictates   – Yours faithfully
        a letter and his   BETA DYNAMICS PLC
        secretary signs on his   (*signature*)
        behalf   pp John Smith
                          Marketing Manager
                        OR
                        Dictated by John Smith
                        and signed in his absence
                        (*signature*)
                        Anna Jones
                        Secretary to Marketing Manager

    c when secretary   – Yours faithfully
       composes a letter and   BETA DYNAMICS PLC
       signs it   *(signature)*
                            Anna Jones
                            Secretary to Mr John Smith
                            Marketing Manager

13 **Enclosures** If enclosures accompany the letter, indicate this by typing 'enc' at the bottom of the letter or by typing the solidus (/) or a line of dots (. . .) in the margin opposite the sentence referring to the enclosure.

14 **Composition** Choose your words carefully and avoid business jargon and unnecessarily long phrases. The following are some examples of phrases to be avoided, together with suggested alternatives:

- I am in receipt of your favour
- I acknowledge receipt of your letter

    – Thank you for your letter, or With reference to your letter

- Please be advised that   – a formal preliminary which is unnecessary
- Referring to the matter   – state the matter
- This is to inform you   – give the information without these preliminary words

- I have enclosed
- Attached please find
- I enclose herewith

    – I enclose

- In view of the fact that   – since
- At this time   – now

Select and use words which express your ideas adequately and with the right amount of emphasis; if a word is used too often it loses its emphasis.

15 **Tone** The tone or language used in a letter will need to be varied according to the nature of the message and the relationship between the correspondents. If you are writing on behalf of your employer, you must adopt the tone which he wishes to be used. It must above all be courteous without failing to express the message clearly. A letter reflects the writer's personality so every opportunity should be taken to give a human and personal impression, even though the letter itself may be typed automatically from a word processor!

16 **Layout** Use the organisation's standard practice for the layout of correspondence. The fully-blocked style is now commonly used but other forms of layout are equally acceptable as long as consistency is maintained throughout. In the fully-blocked layout all lines begin flush at the left-hand margin, as in the example.

Beta Dynamics plc
81 Winterside Road, Weston-Super-Mare, Avon BS24 8AR

Company no: 2464815 England
Telex: 248193 BETACS
Telephone: 0934 27624 Ext 124 ③

② Our Ref: 189/82
Your Ref:

① 1 March 19--

④ The Manager
Queen's Hotel
20 Bloomsbury Square
LONDON   WC1A 4PR

⑧ Dear Sir

⑦ RESERVATION OF ACCOMMODATION

⑩ In confirmation of my telephone conversation today with your
receptionist, Miss P Jarrett, I shall be grateful if you will
reserve a single room with bath for the evenings of 15-18 March
19-- inclusive for Mr J Smith of this company. He would
appreciate a room on the quiet side of the hotel.

I wish to confirm, also, that Mr Smith will be entertaining ten
business associates for dinner at 2000 hrs on 16 March 19--.
He would like you to arrange this in a private room and to serve
cocktails there at 1930 hrs. The meal will be selected by
Mr Smith's guests from the 'à la carte' menu.

All expenses incurred by Mr Smith during his stay at your hotel
will be paid by this company and I shall be glad if you will
forward the account to the above address for my attention.

⑪ Will you please confirm that these arrangements are in order.

⑧ Yours faithfully
BETA DYNAMICS plc

⑫ Anna Jones
Secretary to Mr John Smith
Marketing Manager

A specimen letter

NB: The numbers refer to the key factors in the composition and construction of correspondence.

17 **Punctuation** This is as important as correct facts. The omission of punctuation marks or their incorrect use can

give misleading or wrong impressions. Open punctuation is now common practice for the information above and below the body of the letter, as illustrated in the example, because the punctuation marks do not serve any useful purpose and do not contribute anything to the appearance. An added advantage of open punctuation is the saving of typists' time.

18 **Internal communications** Memos are normally used internally and for communications to branches, agents or representatives in other parts of the country or the world. Salutations and complimentary closes are not used and the inside name and address is usually condensed to the person's name or title. The information in the heading should give:
a name of sender
b name(s) of addressee(s)
c reference
d date
e subject heading

Desk diaries and other memory aids

Key factors in using desk diaries:
1 Be systematic. At the beginning of the day take the necessary action on all entries, eg prepare the papers and files for meetings and appointments. During the course of the day keep in mind and prepare for the various appointments and engagements – make amendments, additions and deletions as required. At the end of the day, ensure that all items have been dealt with or, if necessary, transferred to a future date.
2 Write entries clearly with a pen. Enter provisional appointments in pencil and ink them in when they are confirmed.
3 Appointments for each day should be entered in the correct time sequence.
4 Enter essential details such as full descriptions of appointments, time and place.
5 All entries affecting the employer should be entered in his diary as well as in the secretary's diary (see specimen diaries opposite).

Secretary's Diary

May 19--
17 Monday

1000	Executives Meeting	Boardroom
1130	Appointment (TJM) Mr R W Parker, Conway Engineering Ltd – File 739/82	
1300	TJM – Lunch : Institute of Marketing	Tyrol Restaurant
1500	Interviews for Sales Rep for Wales	Room 100
1900	TJM – Cocktails (with Mrs Mason) at Major Wilson's house	29 Grange Rd
2000	Squash with Betty and Paul	Staff club

NOTES:

Joan Perkins attending Secretarial Development Course
Agenda for Sales Meeting (26 May)

Follow up: Files 812/81
 389/82
 467/82

Employer's Diary
(Mr T J Mason — Marketing Manager)

May 19--
17 Monday

10.00	Executives Meeting	Boardroom
11.30	Mr R W Parker, Conway Engineering Ltd	
13.00	Lunch ~ Institute of Marketing	Tyrol Restaurant
15.00	Interviews for Sales Rep for Wales	Room 100
19.00	Cocktails (with Mrs Mason) at Major Wilson's house	29 Grange Rd

NOTES:

Chief Accountant on holiday (until 24 May)
Paul Pringle ~ 25 yrs with firm on 19 May

(Arrows between the two diaries, labelled centre:)
— Meetings —
— Appointments —
— Luncheon engagements —
— Social engagements —
— Key staff absences —
— Anniversary reminders —
— Work planning —
— Files to be followed up —

Memory aids

The office diary This is the simplest of the aids and one of the most effective methods provided that it is systematically maintained and referred to daily.

Indexed memory aids Index cards or memos are used to record matters which require attention in the future. The system has folders for each day of the month and each month of the year which are stored in a filing cabinet. When a matter requiring attention on a future date arises or when appointments are made, an entry is made on a card or memo and placed in the appropriate folder. The folders are then referred to every day, and after a day's entries have been dealt with, that file is placed at the back of the month's files.

Signalling devices Used in association with visible record cards (see p 47) to highlight the date when the item on a card requires attention.

Plastic year planners Large plastic calendars with spaces for every day of the year can be used for planning appointments, meetings and other business activities. With these you can see at a glance a year's activities and so plan engagements methodically on one single sheet.

Appointments cards An alternative to the office diary for the employer who is away from his office for a whole day, attending various functions and appointments. The card lists the appointments, including time and venue, and is an extract from the diary.

Entertaining in business

The secretary may be involved in the following tasks:

1 Arranging with the firm's catering manager to serve lunch for the employer and his visitors. The catering manager will normally need several days' notice if a special meal is required. After discussing with the catering manager the meal and wine requested by the employer, confirm these in writing together with the date and time.

2 Reserving a table for lunch or dinner at a hotel or restaurant. From his knowledge of the area, the employer will probably suggest the place, otherwise he could be invited to suggest one from a guide such as *Hotel Guide*, the *Good Food Guide* or the *AA Members Handbook*. Telephone in the first place to make sure that a table is available and state the requirements, ie date, time, number of places, and then write a letter to confirm the details.

3 Arranging a dinner party (or cocktail party) – the major tasks include:
   • discussing the function in detail with your employer
   • telephoning and writing a letter booking accommodation and arranging the necessary catering facilities – stating the approximate number of people expected to attend; estimates from several places may have to be obtained before a decision is made
   • printing (or typing) and despatching invitation cards to guests (see specimen invitation card below
   • printing or typing the menu cards or arranging for the caterers to do this for you (see specimen menu card on p 43)
   • when replies have been received, confirming with the caterer the number expected; on the actual day, telephoning the caterer with any last-minute adjustment to the number expected and checking that all arrangements are in hand

---

The Directors and Staff of Computer Accessories PLC
request the pleasure of the company of

....

at a dinner party
to be held at The Country House Hotel, Warwick
on Friday 27 July 19—
1930 for 2000 hrs

RSVP Mrs P Barber, PA to Managing Director, Computer Accessories PLC, Barford, Warwickshire, by 20 July 19—

A specimen invitation card

A selection of common menu terms in French with English translations

French term	English translation
Avocat	Avocado pear
Beignets de langoustines	Scampi
Boeuf bourgignon	Braised beef prepared in red wine with mushrooms and onions
Café	Coffee
Caneton à l'orange	Braised duckling served with orange slices
Cassade	Ice cream with fruit

Choux de Bruxelles	Brussel sprouts served in butter
Consommé	A clear soup
Coq au vin	Chicken prepared in red wine with onions and bacon
Crème anglaise	egg custard
Entrecôte Bercy	Grilled steak served with Bercy butter
Entrecôte maître d'hotel	Grilled steak served with a butter containing chopped parsley and lemon juice
Filet de boeuf	Fillet of beef
Filet de sole meunière	Fillet of sole fried in butter
Fromages	Cheeses
Fruits rafraichis	Fresh fruit salad
Glace	Ice cream
Homard à la nage	Lobster boiled in white wine
Hors d'oeuvres	A starter which may include fish, salads, pâtés, sea foods and snails
Jambon	Ham
Meringue glacée	Ice cream with meringue
Oeuf dur mayonnaise	Hard-boiled egg with mayonnaise
Pâtisserie	A cake or pastry-based sweet
Plat du jour	Special dish of the day
Pointes d'asperges	Asparagus tips
Poire belle Hélène	Ice cream and pears served with a chocolate sauce
Pommes à l'anglaise	Boiled potatoes
Pommes au four	Baked potatoes
Pommes frites	French fried potatoes
Pommes sautées	Sliced potatoes fried in butter
Potage	Soup
Potage aux legumes	Vegetable soup
Poularde rôtie	Roast chicken
Profiteroles	Pastry balls filled with cream
Quiche Lorraine	Savoury flan containing bacon, eggs and cream
Ratatouille	Courgettes, aubergines, tomatoes, green peppers and onions cooked in oil with garlic
Rumsteack grillé	Grilled rump steak
Salade	Salad
Saumon grillé	Grilled salmon
Sorbet	Water ice
Soupe à l'oignon	Onion soup
Tournedos	Small pieces of beef fillet fried in butter or grilled

```
                    COMPUTER ACCESSORIES PLC

                          DINNER PARTY

                          27 July 19—

                              MENU

                         Hors d'oeuvres
                               or
                           Fruit juice
                          ───────

                     Filet de sole meunière
                          ───────

                        Boeuf bourgignon
                           Courgettes
                           Cauliflower
                          New potatoes
                          ───────

                       Poire belle Hélène
                          ───────

                      Cheese and Biscuits
                          ───────

                            Coffee
```

A specimen menu card

Selecting wine to complement food

| Food | Suggested wine | | | | |
	Dry white	Sweet white	Rosé	Red	Port/Madeira
Sea food	x		x		
Fish	x		x		
Chicken	x		x		
Eggs	x		x		
Meat				x	
Casserole dishes				x	
Duck				x	
Pheasant				x	
Guinea fowl				x	
Rabbit				x	
Cheese	x			x	x
Desserts and fruit		x			

NB: Champagne is the only wine that can be served throughout
a meal, complementing all courses.

Filing and indexing glossary of terms

Absent folders/cards Method of controlling and recording files removed from a filing system.

Alphabetical filing Method of classifying files alphabetically by name of correspondent – suitable for correspondence with customers, clients etc in a small/medium-sized organisation.

Box-file Used for storing a limited amount of correspondence when it needs to be kept in a separate container.

Centralised filing All files held in one central office.

Chronological filing Numerical method of filing documents according to their dates.

Computer-assisted retrieval Linking of computer and microfilming systems for rapid retrieval of data. Stages in this process:

a documents for filing are filmed and coded

b key information is entered into the computer as a record which can be accessed on-line or held on a floppy disc for use on a stand-alone computer

c information is retrieved by keying in search details on a terminal keyboard

d information from the computer index is displayed on a VDU

Data Search 1000 for document filming and retrieval

screen which indicates to the operator the appropriate film required

e when the necessary code is keyed in, the required document image is automatically displayed on the screen

f the operator arranges for a 'hard' copy to be printed

Concertina or expanding file Contains a series of pockets which can be opened up like a concertina and papers placed in them for sorting prior to filing.

Cross-referencing Reference in a filing system to the position of a file or card when it is known by more than one name. The cross-reference is placed in the position where the folder or card is not held.

Dead file File which is no longer required for current use.

Decimal filing Numerical classification method used for subject divisions, especially in the arrangement of library books.

Departmental filing Each department holds its own files.

Edge-punched cards These combine a card record system with a rapid process of sorting. The cards are supplied with a series of punched holes round the edges, each representing a specific item of information. The holes are converted into slots to represent relevant data. To select information from the cards, a steel needle is passed through a particular position and any cards which have been slotted in that position fall away from the remainder.

Follow-up system System for bringing forward files to check whether replies have been received to letters sent out.

Geographical filing Files classified alphabetically by geographical location of correspondents – suitable for correspondence with agents or representatives relating to the same area.

Guide cards Used in filing cabinets or index drawers to separate different sections, letters of the alphabet etc to help find files/cards.

Index cards Used for recording and locating information, especially in a numerical method to supply the file numbers.

Lateral filing Files suspended laterally from rails in cabinets, cupboards, racks or shelves (like books on a shelf).

Lever arch file Loose-leaf file where papers are secured by two arch-shaped metal fasteners which are opened and closed by raising or lowering a lever.

Loose-leaf post/prong binders Used for holding stationery with holes punched in it which fit over the posts/prongs. Used especially for filing computer print-out.

Microfilming See p 94.

Miscellaneous file Contains correspondence relating to several subjects/customers which do not have separate files in the system.

Numerical filing Files are allocated numbers and arranged in numerical order – suitable for correspondence with customers, clients etc when a large number of files are involved.

A lateral filing cabinet

Pending file Used to hold daily correspondence and routine papers until acted on.

Plan filing Horizontal or vertical cabinets for filing plans, drawings and large photographs.

Punches Used for punching holes in papers for filing in prong or ring files and binders.

Retention policy Used by an organisation to determine the date when files can be removed from current filing systems and/or destroyed. In deciding this policy, the following factors should be considered:

- volume of correspondence
- frequency of reference required
- access to the information from alternative sources
- audit requirements
- legal requirements

Rotary indexing equipment Indexing unit holding a large number of index cards or line reference strips on a rotating wheel for quick location of information.

Safety first Avoid opening a heavy top drawer of a vertical filing cabinet because the whole cabinet is liable to topple over. It is advisable to open the bottom drawer before the top one so that it serves as a prop and lessens the risk. If possible, load all of the drawers evenly. Do not allow the drawers of filing cabinets and cupboards to protrude into gangways.

Strip indexing Reference data, such as commodity prices, telephone numbers, addresses etc, are recorded on cardboard strips which are built up one above the other in suitable carrying devices so that they are all clearly visible.

Subject filing Files classified alphabetically by subject – suitable for correspondence relating to projects or events where it is important to bring together all papers relating to the same subject.

Terminal digit filing Files arranged according to the last pair of digits of a number instead of the first – only suitable when a very large number of files are involved.

Transfer file File or box for holding documents which have to be kept but are no longer in current use.

Vertical filing Files arranged vertically (upright) in cabinets.

Visible card records Cards held in flat trays overlapping each other but with their edges visible. The visible edges contain 'key' information which can be extracted quickly without handling individual cards, eg file numbers, customer numbers, stock numbers etc.

Suppliers of filing cabinets and accessories

Art Metal Office Equipment PLC, Abbess House, High Street, Southall, Middlesex UB1 3HE

Flexiform Ltd, 16 Duncan Terrace, London N1 8BZ

Rotadex Systems PLC, 3/5 Fortnum Close, Kitts Green, Birmingham B33 0JL

Sankey Sheldon Ltd, 1 Howard Way, Harlow, Essex CM20 2AE

Twinlock PLC, 36 Croydon Road, Beckenham, Kent BR3 4BH

Pointers to efficient filing

1   Ensure that all correspondence has been passed for filing.
2   Sort and group correspondence before filing. A concertina file is useful for this purpose.
3   Remove paper clips before filing correspondence.
4   Check that you are placing correspondence in the correct file.

5 Place papers squarely on the files so that the edges are straight and neat.

6 Arrange the correspondence in chronological order with the most recent on top.

7 Always keep a record if:
   a a document has to be removed from a file
   b a file has to be removed from a cabinet

8 Keep your files up-to-date by filing daily.

9 If a file title is known by more than one name, use cross-references in places where the file is not held.

10 Thin out files regularly in accordance with a file retention policy.

11 Always close filing cabinet drawers after use.

12 Lock filing cabinets before leaving the office at night or for any length of time.

Rules for indexing	*Examples*
1 The surname is placed before the Christian names and, if the surnames are the same, the first Christian name determines the position.	Atkins, James Atkins, John
2 If the Christian name and surname are contained in the name of a firm, the surname is written first, followed by the Christian name and finally by the remainder of the name.	Brown, Peter PLC
3 If a firm has several names, the first is taken as the surname for indexing purposes.	Clarke, Rogers & Arnold
4 The first name is taken in hyphenated names.	Davis, R Ewing-Davis R
5 For impersonal names, such as county councils, use the name that distinguishes it from the others, for indexing purposes.	Hampshire County Council
6 Names beginning with Mac, Mc or M' are treated as if they were spelt 'Mac'.	M'Bride G R McBride P T MacBride W G
7 Names beginning with St are treated as if they were spelt 'Saint'.	St John Courtney Salon Sellers R T

| 8 | Nothing comes before something, ie a name without an initial precedes a name with one. | Thomas
Thomason
Thomason P
Thomason P P |
| 9 | Names which consist of initials are placed before full names | WEA
Watson E A |

First-aid in the office

The law states that all premises must provide an acceptable first-aid box or first-aid cupboard. Where the number of persons employed in the premises exceeds 150 at any one time, an additional box or cupboard must be provided for each unit of 150 persons (or fraction of a unit). Each box or cupboard must:

- contain first-aid requisites and appliances as specified in the Health and Safety (First-Aid) Regulations 1981
- contain no articles other than first-aid requisites and appliances
- be in the charge of a responsible person (no person can be in charge of more than one box or cupboard).

Where the number of persons exceeds 150, at least one must be trained in first-aid treatment and always available during working hours. Notices must be displayed at such posts so that they can be easily seen and read by the employees working in the premises. They must state the names of those who are in charge of the boxes/cupboards and that these persons are always available during working hours. Certain exemptions may, however, be granted where a first-aid room is provided.

When an accident causes loss of life or serious injury or prevents a person from doing his usual work for more than three days, you must notify the Health and Safety Executive, in accordance with the Notification of Accidents and Dangerous Occurrences Regulations 1980.

The importance of first-aid in the office cannot be emphasised too strongly and it is just as important in small offices as it is in large ones. Accidents and illnesses occur in offices of every size, even when elaborate safety precautions are observed. Speedy and proper treatment of injuries and illnesses is essential to protect employees from unnecessary suffering and help them to recover as quickly as possible.

An organisation's first-aid service can only be fully effective when all of its employees:

a are conscious of the need for safety at all times

b know where the nearest first-aid box and facilities are

c know how to contact the named first-aider when an accident or illness occurs

d know how to send quickly for a doctor or an ambulance in major accidents or illnesses

e know how to help an injured person by:

- making the casualty as comfortable as possible (but do not attempt to move the casualty until you know what is wrong)
- ensuring that the casualty can breathe freely – allow plenty of fresh air into the room
- disconnecting the electric power as quickly as possible in the case of an electric shock
- keeping the casualty warm by wrapping her in blankets or coats – for treatment of shock

f know that first-aid treatment, apart from simple procedures such as the above, should only be applied by qualified first-aiders

g complete a detailed report on the incident in accordance with the organisation's policy

Life-saving first-aid measures

Reproduced from the *St John Diary* by kind permission of the St John Ambulance Association.

Avoid becoming a casualty yourself – know the life-saving procedures.

Breathing stopped If the victim stops breathing he will die, unless breathing is restored at once. First tilt his head back to open the air passages from mouth to lungs, squeeze the nostrils together then blow your own breath through his mouth into his lungs.

Bleeding Bleeding from injuries must be controlled as severe loss of blood may lead to death. The best way to stop bleeding is to squeeze the injured part together by direct pressure of the fingers on the wound.

Unconsciousness The willing but untrained bystander is most helpless when confronted with the unconscious victim. The simplest act of turning such a victim on his side, in the recovery position, so that he cannot drown in his own vomit, may save many such victims who would otherwise die.

Shock Shock is likely to be present in all cases of injury and many cases of sudden illness. Its effects which may be extremely serious may be mitigated by the comfort, confidence and reassurance supplied by the rescuer.

Broken bones These are serious injuries – stop any movement of broken bones which may make the injury more severe. Injured limbs may be secured to the body or the other uninjured limb.

Burns and scalds These are common injuries and if a large part of the body is involved death may result. Cool rapidly the affected area with cold water, then cover with clean cloth or large dressing till seen by a doctor.

A thorough knowledge of first aid requires a course of lectures. Details are available from the HQ, St John Ambulance, 1 Grosvenor Crescent, London SW1X 7EF or from the local centre of the association or unit of the brigade. Further information on first aid is supplied in *The First Aid Manual* and *The Digest of First Aid* obtainable from the Supplies Department, Order of St John, Priory House, St John's Gate, Clerkenwell, London EC1.

Flexitime

A method of controlling staff working hours and allowing them to use more flexible starting and leaving times.

In a flexible system there are certain times of the day when all staff are required to be at work. These are known as 'core' times and are usually 1000 to 1200 hours and 1400 to 1600 hours. In addition to these times, staff are required to work a certain number of hours per week or month. These are the flexible hours and can be worked to suit either the convenience of staff or the employer, especially in meeting 'deadlines' for urgent jobs. With people arriving and leaving at different times it is clearly necessary to have some means of recording their individual working hours. There are various methods in use, including:

1 Manually signing a book or filling in time sheets.
2 Using punched card time-recording machines which simultaneously perforate the employee's card and print the time. To help payroll calculations, this machine can be programmed to print normal core time working hours in black and any lateness or overtime in red.
3 Using an electronic control system where staff register their arrivals and departures by inserting a key into the timing device. While the key is inserted they can see the hours and minutes worked to date, including a plus or minus figure showing the time in excess or below the expected time. A print-out is available at the end of the period for calculating pay and for the information of departmental managers.

Features of the flexitime system:
1 Staff plan their times of arrival and departure to fit in with their domestic circumstances and, as a result, are able to concentrate better on their work. This is particularly beneficial for married women with young children to take and collect from school.
2 There is less traffic congestion as staff arrive and leave at different times.
3 The occasional day or half-day's leave can be earned by working longer hours for a previous period.

Foreign countries

Country	Capital	Nationality	Official language
Afghanistan	Kabul	Afghan	Persian, Pushtu
Albania	Tirana	Albanian	Albanian
Algeria	Algiers	Algerian	Arabic, French
Andorra	Andorra La Vella	Andorran	Catalan
Angola	Luanda	Angolan	Portuguese
Argentina	Buenos Aires	Argentine	Spanish
Australia	Canberra	Australian	English
Austria	Vienna	Austrian	German
Azores	Ponta Delgada	Azorean	Portuguese
Bahamas	Nassau	Bahamian	English
Bahrain	Manama	Bahraini	Arabic
Bangladesh	Dacca	Bengali	Bengali
Barbados	Bridgetown	Barbadian	English
Belgium	Brussels	Belgian	Flemish, French
Belize	Belmopan	Belizean	English, Spanish
Bermuda	Hamilton	Bermudian	English
Bolivia	La Paz	Bolivian	Spanish
Brazil	Brasilia	Brazilian	Portuguese
Brunei	Banda Seri Begawan	Bruneian	English, Malay
Bulgaria	Sofia	Bulgarian	Bulgarian
Burma	Rangoon	Burmese	Burmese
Burundi	Bujumbura	Burundian	French, Rundi
Cameroon	Yaoundé	Cameroonian	English, French

4 Staff are aware of the need to plan their time effectively throughout the day.
5 Time-keeping is more effectively controlled and fewer lateness and absence problems occur.
6 Staff are more willing to work overtime to alleviate peaks of work and to meet 'deadlines'.
7 A disadvantage is that internal communication is less effective outside 'core' times when staff may not be in their offices.

Currency unit	Currency symbol	High Commission/ Embassy address in London	Country
Afghani	Af	31 Princes Gate, SW7 1QQ	Afghanistan
Lek	L	—	Albania
Dinar	DA	54 Holland Park, W11 3RS	Algeria
Fr Franc	F	—	Andorra
Sp Peseta	P	—	
Kwanza	Kz	—	Angola
Peso	$	9 Wilton Crescent, SW1X 0LB	Argentina
Dollar	$	Australia House, Strand, WC2R 3ER	Australia
Schilling	S	18 Belgrave Mews West, SW1X 8BU	Austria
Escudo	$	—	Azores
Dollar	B$	39 Pall Mall, SW1Y 5JG	Bahamas
Dinar	BD	98 Gloucester Road, SW7 4AU	Bahrain
Taka	Tk	28 Queen's Gate, SW7 5JA	Bangladesh
Dollar	$	6 Upper Belgrave Street, SW1X 8AZ	Barbados
Franc	F	103 Eaton Square, SW1W 9AB	Belgium
Dollar	$	—	Belize
Dollar	$	—	Bermuda
Peso	$B	106 Eaton Square, SW1W 9AB	Bolivia
Cruzeiro	Cr$	32 Green Street, W1Y 5LH	Brazil
Dollar	$	—	Brunei
Lev	Lv	186 Queen's Gate Gardens, SW7 5HL	Bulgaria
Kyat	K	19A Charles Street, Berkeley Square, W1X 8ER	Burma
Franc	FBu	—	Burundi
Franc	F	84 Holland Park, W11 3SB	Cameroon

Country	Capital	Nationality	Official language
Canada	Ottawa	Canadian	English, French
Canary Islands	Tenerife	Canarian	English, Spanish
Chile	Santiago	Chilian	Spanish
China	Peking	Chinese	Chinese
Colombia	Bogotá	Colombian	Spanish
Congo	Brazzaville	Congolese	French
Costa Rica	San José	Costa Rican	Spanish
Cuba	Havana	Cuban	Spanish
Cyprus	Nicosia	Cypriot	Greek, Turkish
Czechoslovakia	Prague	Czechoslovak	Czech, Slovak
Denmark	Copenhagen	Danish	Danish
Dominican Republic	Canto Domingo	Dominican	Spanish
Ecuador	Quito	Ecuadorean	Spanish
Egypt	Cairo	Egyptian	Arabic
Ethiopia	Addis Ababa	Ethiopian	Amharic
Fiji	Suva	Fijian	English
Finland	Helsinki	Finnish	Finnish
France	Paris	French	French
Gabon	Libreville	Gabonese	French
Gambia	Banjul	Gambian	English
Germany, East	East Berlin	East German	German
Germany, West	Bonn	West German	German
Ghana	Accra	Ghanaian	English
Greece	Athens	Greek	Greek
Grenada	St Georges	Grenadian	English
Guatemala	Guatemala City	Guatemalan	Spanish
Guinea	Conakry	Guinean	French
Guyana	Georgetown	Guyanese	English
Haiti	Port-au-Prince	Haitian	French
Honduras	Tegucigalpa	Honduran	Spanish
Hong Kong	Victoria	Hong Kong	English, Cantonese
Hungary	Budapest	Hungarian	Hungarian
Iceland	Reykjavik	Icelandic	Icelandic

Currency unit	Currency symbol	High Commission/ Embassy address in London	Country
Dollar	$	Macdonald House, 1 Grosvenor Square, W1X 0AA	**Canada**
Peseta	P	—	**Canary Islands**
Peso	$	12 Devonshire Street, W1N 1FS	**Chile**
Yuan	$	31 Portland Place, W1N 3AG	**China**
Peso	$	3 Hans Crescent, SW1X 0LB	**Colombia**
Franc	F	—	**Congo**
Colon	₡	Cromwell Mansions, 225 Cromwell Road, SW5 0RX	**Costa Rica**
Peso	$	167 High Holborn, WC1 8AB	**Cuba**
Pound	£	93 Park Street, W1Y 4ET	**Cyprus**
Koruna	Kčs	25 Kensington Palace Gardens, W8 4QY	**Czechoslovakia**
Krone	Kr	55 Sloane Street, SW1X 9SR	**Denmark**
Peso	RD$	4 Braemar Mansions, Cornwall Gardens, SW7 4AQ	**Dominican Republic**
Sucre	S/	Flat 3B, 3 Hans Crescent, SW1X 0LS	**Ecuador**
Pound	£E	26 South Street, W1Y 4ET	**Egypt**
Dollar	E$	17 Prince's Gate, SW7 1PZ	**Ethiopia**
Dollar	$F	34 Hyde Park Gate, SW7 5BN	**Fiji**
Markka	M	38 Chesham Place, SW1X 8HW	**Finland**
Franc	F	11 Kensington Palace Gardens, W8 4QY	**France**
Franc	F	48 Kensington Court, W8 5DB	**Gabon**
Dalasi	D	60 Ennismore Gardens, SW7 1NH	**Gambia**
Ostmark	OM	34 Belgrave Square, SW1X 8QB	**Germany, East**
Deutschemark	DM	23 Belgrave Square, SW1X 8PZ	**Germany, West**
Cedi	₡	13 Belgrave Square, SW1X 8PZ	**Ghana**
Drachma	Dr	1a Holland Park, W11 3TP	**Greece**
Dollar	$	102 Grand Buildings, Trafalgar Square, WC2B 8BQ	**Grenada**
Quetzal	Q	—	**Guatemala**
Syli	Sy	—	**Guinea**
Dollar	G$	3 Palace Court, Bayswater Road, W2 4LP	**Guyana**
Gourde	G	11 Queen's Gate, SW7 5JA	**Haiti**
Lempira	L	48 George Street, W1H 5RF	**Honduras**
Dollar	HK$	6 Grafton Street, W1X 3LB	**Hong Kong**
Forint	Ft	35 Eaton Place, SW1W 9AB	**Hungary**
Krona	Kr	1 Eaton Terrace, SW1W 8EY	**Iceland**

Country	Capital	Nationality	Official language
India	New Delhi	Indian	English, Hindi
Indonesia	Jakarta	Indonesian	Indonesian
Iran	Tehran	Iranian	Persian
Iraq	Baghdad	Iraqi	Arabic
Ireland (Eire)	Dublin	Irish	Irish, English
Israel	Jerusalem	Israeli	Hebrew, Arabic
Italy	Rome	Italian	Italian
Ivory Coast	Abidjan	Ivory Coaster	French
Jamaica	Kingston	Jamaican	English
Japan	Tokyo	Japanese	Japanese
Jordan	Amman	Jordanian	Arabic
Kampuchea (Cambodia)	Phnom Penh	Kampuchean	Kampuchean
Kenya	Nairobi	Kenyan	English, Swahili
Korea (North)	Pyongyang	North Korean	Korean
Korea (South)	Seoul	South Korean	Korean
Kuwait	Kuwait City	Kuwaiti	Arabic
Laos	Vientiane	Laotian	Lao
Lesotho	Maseru	Basotho	English
Liberia	Monrovia	Liberian	English
Libya	Tripoli	Libyan	Arabic
Liechtenstein	Vaduz	Liechtensteiner	German
Luxembourg	Luxembourg City	Luxembourger	French, German
Macau	Macau	Macauan	Portuguese, Cantonese, English
Malagasy (Madagascar)	Tananarive	Malagasy	French, Malagasy
Malawi	Lilongwe	Malawian	English, Nyanja
Malaysia	Kuala Lumpur	Malaysian	Malay
Maldive Islands	Male	Maldivian	Maldivian
Mali	Bamako	Malian	French
Malta	Valletta	Maltese	English, Maltese
Mauritania	Nouakchott	Mauritanian	Arabic, French
Mauritius	Port Louis	Mauritian	English
Mexico	Mexico City	Mexican	Spanish

Currency unit	Currency symbol	High Commission/ Embassy address in London	Country
Rupee	Re	India House, Aldwych, WC2B 4NA	India
Rupiah	Rp	38 Grosvenor Square, W1X 9AD	Indonesia
Rial	R	26 Princes Gate, SW7 1QQ	Iran
Dinar	ID	21 Queen's Gate, SW7 5JG	Iraq
Punt	£	17 Grosvenor Place, SW1X 7HR	Ireland (Eire)
Shekel	IS	2 Palace Green, Kensington, W8 4QB	Israel
Lira	L	14 Three Kings Yard, Davies Street, W1X 2DQ	Italy
Franc	F	2 Upper Belgrave Street, SW1X 8BJ	Ivory Coast
Dollar	$	50 St James's Street, SW1A 1JT	Jamaica
Yen	Y	43 Grosvenor Street, W1X 0BA	Japan
Dinar	JD	6 Chester Terrace, NW1	Jordan
Riel	CR	—	Kampuchea (Cambodia)
Shilling	Sh	45 Portland Place, W1N 4AS	Kenya
Won	W	—	Korea (North)
Won	W	4 Palace Gate, W8 5NF	Korea (South)
Dinar	KD	45 Queen's Gate, SW7 5JA	Kuwait
Kip	K	5 Palace Green, W8 4QA	Laos
Rand	R	16A St James's Street, SW1A 1EU	Lesotho
Dollar	$	21 Prince's Gate, SW7 1QB	Liberia
Dinar	LD	5 St James's Square, SW1A 1JJ	Libya
Sw. Franc	F	—	Liechtenstein
Franc	F	27 Wilton Crescent, SW1X 8SD	Luxembourg
Pataca	P	—	Macau
Franc	F	—	Malagasy (Madagascar)
Kwacha	K	33 Grosvenor Street, W1X 0HS	Malawi
Dollar	M$	45 Belgrave Square, SW1X 8QT	Malaysia
Rupee	Re	—	Maldive Islands
Franc	F	—	Mali
Pound	£	24 Haymarket, SW1Y 4DJ	Malta
Ouguiya	O	—	Mauritania
Rupee	Re	32 Elvaston Place, SW7 5HL	Mauritius
Peso	$	8 Halkin Street, SW1X 7DW	Mexico

Country	Capital	Nationality	Official language
Monaco	Monte Carlo	Monegasque/ Monacan	French
Mongolia	Ulan Bator	Mongol	Mongolian
Mozambique	Maputo	Mozambican	Portuguese
Nepal	Katmandu	Nepalese	Nepali
Netherlands (Holland)	The Hague	Dutch	Dutch
New Zealand	Wellington	New Zealander	English
Nicaragua	Managua	Nicaraguan	Spanish
Niger	Niamey	Nigerois	French
Nigeria	Lagos	Nigerian	English
Norway	Oslo	Norwegian	Norwegian
Oman	Muscat	Omani	Arabic
Pakistan	Islamabad	Pakistani	Bengali, English, Urdu
Panama	Panama City	Panamanian	Spanish
Papua New Guinea	Port Moresby	Papua New Guinean	English
Paraguay	Asuncion	Paraguayan	Spanish
Peru	Lima	Peruvian	Spanish
Philippines	Quezon City	Filipino	English, Pilipino
Poland	Warsaw	Polish	Polish
Portugal	Lisbon	Portuguese	Portuguese
Puerto Rico	San Juan	Puerto Rican	English, Spanish
Qatar	Doha	Qatari	Arabic
Romania	Bucharest	Romanian	Romanian
Rwanda	Kigali	Rwandan	French, Ruada
San Marino	San Marino	San Marinese	Italian
Sao Tome & Principe	Sao Tome	Sao Tomean	Portuguese
Saudi Arabia	Riyadh	Saudi Arabian	Arabic
Senegal	Dakar	Senegalese	French
Seychelles	Victoria	Seychellois	English
Sierra Leone	Freetown	Sierra Leonean	English
Singapore	Singapore	Singaporean	Chinese, English, Malay, Tamil
Somalia	Mogadishu	Somali	Somali

Currency unit	Currency symbol	High Commission/ Embassy address in London	Country
Fr. Franc	F	4 Audley Square, W1Y 5DR	Monaco
Tugrik	T	7 Kensington Court, W8 5DL	Mongolia
Escudo	Esc	—	Mozambique
Rupee	Re	12A Kensington Palace Gardens, W8 4QU	Nepal
Guilder	G	38 Hyde Park Gate, SW7 5DP	Netherlands (Holland)
Dollar	NZ$	New Zealand House, Haymarket, SW1Y 4TQ	New Zealand
Cordoba	C$	8 Gloucester Road, SW7 4PP	Nicaragua
Franc	F	—	Niger
Naira	₦	Nigeria House, 9 Northumberland Avenue, WC2	Nigeria
Krone	Kr	25 Belgrave Square, SW1X 8QD	Norway
Rial	R	63 Ennismore Gardens, SW7 5DN	Oman
Rupee	Re	35 Lowndes Square, SW1X 9JN	Pakistan
Balbao	B	Eagle House, 109 Jermyn Street, SW1X 1AB	Panama
Kina	K	14 Waterloo Place, SW1R 4AR	Papua New Guinea
Guarani	G	Braemer Lodge, Cornwall Gardens, SW7 4AQ	Paraguay
Sol	S	52 Sloane Street, SW1X 9SP	Peru
Peso	P	9a Palace Green, W8 4QA	Philippines
Zloty	Z	47 Portland Place, W1N 4EA	Poland
Escudo	Esc	11 Belgrave Square, SW1X 8QB	Portugal
US Dollar	$	—	Puerto Rico
Riyal	R	27 Chesham Place, SW1X 8HH	Qatar
Leu	L	4 Palace Green, W8 4QD	Romania
Franc	F	—	Rwanda
Lira	L	Saxone House, 74A Regent Street, W1Y 4ET	San Marino
Escudo	Esc	—	Sao Tome & Principe
Riyal	SR	30 Belgrave Square, SW1X 8QB	Saudi Arabia
Franc	F	11 Phillimore Gardens, W8 7QG	Senegal
Rupee	Re	2 Mill Street, W1N 3BG	Seychelles
Leone	Le	33 Portland Place, W1N 3AG	Sierra Leone
Dollar	S$	2 Wilton Crescent, SW1X 8ND	Singapore
Shilling	Sh	60 Portland Place, W1N 3DG	Somalia

Country	Capital	Nationality	Official language
South Africa	Pretoria (Administrative) Bloemfontein (Judicial) Capetown (Legislative)	South African	Afrikaans, English
Spain	Madrid	Spanish	Spanish
Sri Lanka	Colombo	Sri Lankan	Sinhalese
Sudan	Khartoum	Sudanese	Arabic
Surinam	Paramaribo	Surinamese	Dutch
Swaziland	Mbabane	Swazi	English
Sweden	Stockholm	Swedish	Swedish
Switzerland	Berne	Swiss	French, German, Italian, Romansh
Syria	Damascus	Syrian	Arabic
Tanzania	Dar es Salaam	Tanzanian	English, Swahili
Thailand	Bangkok	Thai	Thai
Togo	Lomé	Togolese	French
Tonga	Nukualofa	Tongan	English, Tongan
Trinidad & Tobago	Port of Spain	Trinidadian and Tobagonian	English
Tunisia	Tunis	Tunisian	Arabic
Turkey	Ankara	Turkish	Turkish
Uganda	Kampala	Ugandan	English
United Arab Emirates	Abu Dhabi	Arabic	Arabic
United States of America (USA)	Washington DC	American	English
Union of Soviet Socialist Republics (USSR)	Moscow	Russian	Russian
Upper Volta	Ouagagougou	Upper Voltan	French
Uruguay	Montevideo	Uruguayan	Spanish
Venezuela	Caracas	Venezuelan	Spanish
Vietnam	Hanoi	Vietnamese	Vietnamese
Western Samoa	Apia	Western Samoan	English, Samoan
Yemen (South)	Aden	Yemeni	Arabic, English
Yemen (Arab Republic)	Sana	Yemeni	Arabic

Currency unit	Currency symbol	High Commission/ Embassy address in London	Country
Rand	R	South Africa House, Trafalgar Square, WC2B 8QT	**South Africa**
Peseta	P	24 Belgrave Square, SW1X 8PZ	**Spain**
Rupee	Re	13 Hyde Park Gardens, W2 2LU	**Sri Lanka**
Pound	£S	3 Cleveland Row, SW1A 1DD	**Sudan**
Guilder	G	—	**Surinam**
Lilangeni	E	58 Pont Street, SW1X 0AE	**Swaziland**
Krona	Kr	27 Portland Place, W1R 2DN	**Sweden**
Franc	F	16 Montagu Place, W1H 2BQ	**Switzerland**
Pound	£S	8 Belgrave Square, SW1X 8PH	**Syria**
Shilling	Sh	43 Hertford Street, W1Y 7TF	**Tanzania**
Baht	B	30 Queen's Gate, SW7 5JB	**Thailand**
Franc	F	20 Wellington Court, 116 Knightsbridge, SW1X 8PH	**Togo**
Pa'anga	T$	New Zealand House, Haymarket, SW1Y 4TE	**Tonga**
Dollar	TT$	42 Belgrave Square, SW1X 8NT	**Trinidad & Tobago**
Dinar	D	29 Prince's Gate, SW7 1QG	**Tunisia**
Lira	LT	43 Belgrave Square, SW1X 8NT	**Turkey**
Shilling	Sh	—	**Uganda**
Dirham	DH	30 Prince's Gate, SW7 1PT	**United Arab Emirates**
Dollar	$	Grosvenor Square, W1A 2JB	**United States of America (USA)**
Rouble	R	13 Kensington Palace Gardens, W8 4QS	**Union of Soviet Socialist Republics (USSR)**
Franc	F	—	**Upper Volta**
Peso	$	48 Lennox Gardens, SW1X 0DL	**Uruguay**
Bolivar	B	1 Cromwell Road, SW7 2ED	**Venezuela**
Dong	D	12 Victoria Road, W8 5JU	**Vietnam**
Tala	WS$	—	**Western Samoa**
Dinar	£SY	57 Cromwell Road, SW7 2ED	**Yemen (South)**
Riyal	YR	41 South Street, W1Y 5PD	**Yemen (Arab Republic)**

Country	Capital	Nationality	Official language
Yugoslavia	Belgrade	Yugoslav	Macedonian, Serbo-Croatian, Slovenian
Zaire	Kinshasa	Zairian	French
Zambia	Lusaka	Zambian	English
Zimbabwe	Harare	Zimbabwean	English

Forms of address

The table of forms of address which follows is a selection of those in common use. A more comprehensive collection can be found in *Black's Titles and Forms of Address* or, if you want further information concerning protocol and the correct methods of addressing public dignitaries, you can apply to the Protocol Office at the Foreign and Commonwealth Office, King Charles Street, Whitehall, London SW1A 2AH (telephone: 01 233 3000).

The forms of address given are appropriate for formal correspondence, but less formal expressions may be used, depending on the relationship of the writers. A secretary should have a clear understanding with her boss concerning any departure from formal practice. Decorations, honours and qualifications should be included after a correspondent's name, usually in the order of their importance in the following sequence (see p 63):

Title	Form of address
Ambassador – British	His Excellency, Her Britannic Majesty's Ambassador and Plenipotentiary
Ambassador – foreign	His Excellency, The (name of country) Ambassador, or The Honourable (name of country) Ambassador

Currency unit	Currency symbol	High Commission/ Embassy address in London	Country
Dinar	Din	5 Lexham Gardens, W8 5JU	**Yugoslavia**
Zaire	Z	26 Chesham Place, SW1X 8HH	**Zaire**
Kwacha	K	7 Cavendish Place, W1N 0HB	**Zambia**
Dollar	$	Zimbabwe House, Strand, WC2R 0SA	**Zimbabwe**

1	**Decorations and honours**	– CB	Companion of the Bath
		CBE	Commander of the British Empire
		DSO	Distinguished Service Order
2	**Qualifications**	– PhD	Doctor of Philosophy
		MA	Master of Arts
		BA	Bachelor of Arts
3	**Titles relating to membership of professional bodies**	– ACA	Associate of the Institute of Chartered Accountants
		AMBIM	Associate Member of the British Institute of Management
4	**Other titles**	– MP	Member of Parliament
		JP	Justice of the Peace

Examples:
Air Vice Marshal SC Canning, CB, BSc, AMBIM, JP
Miss P Walker, MBE, MA, MP

Salutation		Complimentary close
Sir Your Grace My Lord	according to title	I am, Sir (as appropriate to title) Your obedient servant
Your Excellency		I have the honour to be, Sir, Yours faithfully

Title	Form of address
Archbishop – Anglican	His Grace the Lord Archbishop of –
Archbishop – Roman Catholic	The Most Reverend –, Archbishop of –
Archdeacon	The Venerable the Archdeacon of –
Baron	The Rt Hon Lord –
Baroness	The Rt Hon Lady –
Baronet	Sir – Bt
Baronet's wife	Lady –
Bishop (with seat in Lords)	The Right Rev the Lord Bishop of –
Bishop (not in Lords)	The Right Rev the Bishop of –
Bishop (Roman Catholic)	The Right Rev the Lord Bishop of –
Canon	The Very Reverend Canon –
Cardinal	His Eminence Cardinal –
Clergyman	The Rev –
Consul	(Name) Esq Her Britannic Majesty's Consul General
Countess	The Rt Hon The Countess of –
Dame	Dame – DBE (or appropriate title)
Duchess	Her Grace the Duchess of –
Duke	His Grace the Duke of –
Earl	The Right Hon the Earl of –
Judge (County Court)	His Honour Judge –
Judge (High Court)	The Honourable Mr Justice –
Justice of the Peace	(Name) Esq JP
Knight	Sir – Kt (or appropriate title)
Knight's wife	Lady –
Lord Mayor	The Right Worshipful the Lord Mayor of –

Salutation	Complimentary close
My Lord Archbishop	I have the honour to be, My Lord Archbishop, Your Lordship's obedient servant
My Lord Archbishop	I have the honour to be, My Lord Archbishop, Your Grace's devoted and obedient child ('servant' may be substituted for 'child' by non-Catholics)
Venerable Sir	Yours faithfully
My Lord	I have the honour to be, my Lord, Your Ladyship's obedient servant
Madam	I have the honour to be, Madam, Your ladyship's obedient servant
Sir	I am, Sir, Your obedient servant
Madam	I am, Madam, Your obedient servant
My Lord Bishop	I have the honour to be, My Lord Bishop, Your obedient servant
Sir	I am, Sir, Your obedient servant
My Lord Bishop	I am, Sir, Your obedient child (servant)
Very Reverend Canon, or Dear Canon	Yours faithfully
My Lord Cardinal	I have the honour to be, Your Eminence's obedient servant
Dear Sir	I am, Sir, Your obedient servant, or Yours faithfully
Sir	I am, Sir, Your obedient servant
Madam	I have the honour to be, Madam, Your Ladyship's obedient servant
Dear Madam	Yours faithfully
Madam	I am, Madam, Your Grace's most obedient servant
My Lord Duke	I am, my Lord Duke, Your Grace's most obedient servant
My Lord	I have the honour to be, my Lord, Your Lordship's obedient servant
Sir	I am, Sir, Your obedient servant
Sir	I am, Sir, Your obedient servant
Dear Sir	Yours faithfully
Sir	I am, Sir, Your obedient servant
Madam	I am, Madam, Your obedient servant
My Lord Mayor	I am, My Lord Mayor, Your obedient servant

Title	Form of address
Lord Mayor's wife	The Lady Mayoress of –
Lord Provost	The Lord Provost of –
Mayor	The Worshipful Mayor of –
Mayoress	The Mayoress of –
Member of Parliament	According to rank or title, but with the addition of the letters MP after the name
Officers of the Armed Forces	(1) Rank (2) Title (if any) (3) Name eg Air Vice Marshal Sir Robert Price, KBE DFC
Pope	His Holiness Pope –
Prime Minister	The Right Honourable – PC, MP
Privy Councillor (not being also a peer) and Cabinet Ministers	The Rt Hon – PC, MP
Her Majesty the Queen	Her Most Gracious Majesty, Queen Elizabeth II
Viscount	The Rt Hon the Viscount –
Viscountess	The Rt Hon the Viscountess –

Forms of address for letters to Europe

Country		Form of address
France:	men	M –
	married women	Mme –
	unmarried women	Mlle –
Germany:	men	Herrn –
	married women	Frau –
	unmarried women	Fräulein –
Italy:	Men	Gentilissimo Signore –, or Egregio Signore
	married women	Distinta Signora –
	unmarried women	Esimia Signorina –
Spain:	men	Señor –
	married women	Señora –
	unmarried women	Señorita –

Salutation	Complimentary close
My Lady Mayoress	I am, My Lady Mayoress, Your obedient servant
My Lord Provost	I am, My Lord Provost, Your obedient servant
Sir	I am, Sir, Your obedient servant
Madam	I am, Madam, Your obedient servant
Dear Sir	Yours faithfully
Sir, or Dear (rank)	Yours faithfully or as appropriate to rank
Your Holiness, or Most Holy Father	I have the honour to be Your Holiness's most devoted and obedient child (servant)
Madam/Sir	I have the honour to be, Madam/Sir, Your obedient servant
Madam/Sir	I am, Madam/Sir, Your obedient servant
Madam	I have the honour to be, Madam, Your Majesty's faithful subject
My Lord	I am, My Lord, Your obedient servant
Madam	I have the honour to be, Madam, Your Ladyship's obedient servant

Salutation	Complimentary close
Monsieur Madame Mademoiselle or Madame	Avec mes meilleurs sentiments
Sehr geehrter Herr Sehr geehrte Frau Sehr geehrtes Fräulein	Mit Freundlichem Gruss
Gentilissimo Signore, or Egregio Signore Distinta Signora Esimia Signorina	Cordiali saluti
Muy Señor Mio Muy Estimada Señora Muy Distinguida Señorita	le saluda atentamente

Government departments

Department	Address	Telephone no
Advisory, Conciliation and Arbitration Service	Cleland House, Page Street, London SW1P 4LT	01 211 3000
Ministry of Agriculture, Fisheries and Food	Whitehall Place, London SW1A 2HH	01 839 7711
British Airports Authority	2 Buckingham Gate, London SW1E 6JL	01 834 6621
British Broadcasting Corporation	Broadcasting House, London W1A 1AA	01 580 4468
The British Council	10 Spring Gardens, London SW1A 2BN	01 930 8466
British Gas Corporation	59 Bryanston Street, London W1H 7AR	01 723 7030
British Railways Board	Euston Square, PO Box 100, London NW1 1DH	01 262 3232
British Steel Corporation	33 Grosvenor Place, London SW1X 7JG	01 235 1212
British Tourist Authority	Queen's House, 64 St James's Street, London SW1A 1NF	01 629 9191
British Transport Docks Board	Melbury House, Melbury Terrace, London NW1 6LA	01 486 6621
British Waterways Board	Melbury House, Melbury Terrace, London NW1 6LA	01 262 6711
Civil Aviation Authority	CAA House, 43 Kingsway, London WC2B 6TE	01 379 7311
Civil Service Department	Whitehall, London SW1A 2AZ	01 273 3000
Commonwealth Development Corporation	33 Hill Street, London W1A 3AR	01 629 8484
Board of Customs and Excise	King's Beam House, Mark Lane, London EC3R 7AR	01 626 1515
Department of Education and Science	Elizabeth House, York Road, London SE1 7PH	01 928 9222
The Electricity Council	30 Millbank, London SW1P 4RD	01 834 2333
Department of Employment	Caxton House, Tothill Street, London SW1H 9NA	01 213 3000
Department of Energy	Thames House South, Millbank, London SW1P 4QE	01 211 3000
Department of the Environment	2 Marsham Street, London SW1P 3EB	01 212 3434
Equal Opportunities Commission	Overseas House, Quay Street, Manchester M3 3HN	061 833 9244
Export Credits Guarantee Department	PO Box 272, Aldermanbury House, Aldermanbury, London EC2V 7HP	01 606 6699
Office of Fair Trading	Field House, Bream's Buildings, London EC4A 1HA	01 242 2858
Foreign and Commonwealth Office	Downing Street, London SW1A 2AL	01 233 3000
Department of Health and Social Security	Alexander Fleming House, Elephant and Castle, London SE1 6TB	01 407 5522

Department	Address	Telephone no
Industrial Injuries Advisory Council	Keysign House, 429 Oxford Street, London W1R 1FJ	01 499 4040
Home Office	50 Queen Anne's Gate, London SW1H 9AP	01 213 3000
Independent Broadcasting Authority	70 Brompton Road, London SW3 1HA	01 584 7011
Department of Industry	Ashdown House, 123 Victoria Street, London SW1E 5LT	01 212 7676
Departments of Industry and Trade – Common Services	1 Victoria Street, London SW1H 0EX	01 215 7877
Central Office of Information	Hercules Road, London SE1 7DP	01 928 2345
Board of Inland Revenue	Somerset House, London WC2R 1LB	01 438 6622
Manpower Services Commission	Selkirk House, 166 High Holborn, London WC1V 7JJ	01 836 1213
Monopolies and Mergers Commission	New Court, 48 Carey Street, London WC2A 2JT	01 831 6111
The Commonwealth Institute	Kensington High Street, London W8 6NQ	01 602 3252
National Coal Board	Hobart House, Grosvenor Place, London SW1X 7AE	01 235 2020
National Economic Development Office	Millbank Tower, Millbank, London SW1P 4QX	01 211 3000
National Enterprise Board	12 Grosvenor Gardens, London SW1W 0DH	01 730 9600
National Freight Corporation	Argosy House, 215 Great Portland Street, London W1A 3DG	01 636 8688
Northern Ireland Office	Great George Street, London SW1P 3AJ	01 233 3000
	Stormont House, Belfast BT4 3ST	0232 63255
Ordnance Survey	Romsey Road, Maybush, Southampton SO1 4BY	0703 775555
Office of the Parliamentary Commissioner and Health Service Commissioner	Church House, Great Smith Street, London SW1P 3BW	01 212 7676
Patent Office	25 Southampton Buildings, London WC2E 7HB	01 405 8721
The Post Office	23 Howland Street, London W1P 5FF	01 631 2345
Scottish Office	Dover House, Whitehall, London SW1A 2AU	01 233 5787
	New St Andrew's House, St James Centre, Edinburgh EH1 3SS	031 556 8400
Her Majesty's Stationery Office	Sovereign House, Botolph Street, Norwich NR3 1DN	0603 22211
Department of Trade	1 Victoria Street, London SW1H 0ET	01 215 7877
Export Services and Promotions Division	Export House, 50 Ludgate Hill, London EC4M 7HX	01 248 5757
Companies Registration Office	Companies House, Crown Way, Maindy, Cardiff CF4 3UT	0222 388588
Registry of Business Names	55 City Road, London EC1Y 1AU	01 253 9393

Department	Address	Telephone no
Department of Transport	2 Marsham Street, London SW1P 4JQ	01 212 3434
Welsh Office	Gwydyr House, Whitehall, London SW1A 2ER	01 233 3000
	Cathays Park, Cardiff CF1 3NQ	0222 825111

Industrial Training Boards

Industry	Address
Clothing and Allied Products	Tower House, Merrion Way, Leeds LS2 8PF
Construction	Radnor House, London Road, Norbury, London SW16 4DQ
Engineering	54 Clarendon Road, Watford, Herts WD1 1HA
Hotel and Catering	Ramsey House, Central Square, Wembley, Middx HA9 7AP
Petroleum	Kingfisher House, Walton Street, Aylesbury, Bucks HP20 1TZ
Road Transport	Capitol House, Empire Way, Wembley, Middx HA9 0NG
Rubber and Plastics Processing	Brent House, 950 Great West Road, Brentford, Middx TW8 9ES

Holiday rota

Important factors to consider when organising a staff holiday rota:

1 Start planning in the autumn preceding the year in question to give staff the opportunity to book their holidays in good time and to allow time for discussion and consultation.
2 Give staff as much choice as possible for their holiday dates but have regard to the following constraints:
   a continuity of office services throughout the year; it is essential to have adequate cover at different staff levels, eg supervisory, senior secretarial, typing and reception
   b if there are set dates for the factory employees to take their holidays, the majority of office staff should be encouraged to choose the same dates, retaining a 'skeleton' staff only
   c the fluctuating work cycle, ie fewer staff should be away when there is known to be a peak load of work

Holiday rota 19—

Name	Position	June 1	June 8	June 15	June 22	June 29*	July 6	July 13	July 20*	July 27	Aug 3	Aug 10	Aug 17	Aug 24	Aug 31*	Sept 7	Sept 14	Sept 21	Sept 28*
J Brown	Supervisor	x					x				x								
R Williams	Asst Supervisor				x									x			x		
R Platt	Senior secretary		x							x			x						
T Davies	Senior secretary			x						x	x						x		
R Fox	Shorthand typist							x		x						x			
T Grant	Shorthand typist						x					x							
M Neal	Word processing operator									x	x		x					x	
C May	Receptionist/telephonist		x		x				x							x			
J Gould	Receptionist/telephonist			x							x				x				
T Clark	Reprographics operator									x	x								
Total staff absent		1	2	2	2	0	2	1	1	5	5	1	2	1	1	2	2	1	0

Weeks commencing

Notes: 50 per cent of staff are taking holidays during the works holiday, ie 27 July and 3 August.
* Peak work loads occur in these weeks – staff absences reduced to a minimum.
Assistant Supervisor deputises for Supervisor.
Shorthand typist covers for word processing operator.
Receptionist/telephonist covers for reprographics operator.

3 Managers/supervisors should be asked to approve holiday dates for staff in their departments.
4 Use a chart, such as the one on p 71, to plot the dates when staff are on holiday.
5 If holidays are taken for periods of less than a week, a different type of aid should be used, such as a plastic year planner. This provides spaces for every day of the year and different coloured plastic markers can be used for various staff categories.

Information sources

Information	Source of reference
1 Governmental	
Governments for countries throughout the world and international organisations	– *Statesman's Year Book*
Local government authorities	– *Municipal Year Book and Public Services Directory*
Members of Parliament	– *Times Guide to the House of Commons*
News reference service	– *Keesing's Contemporary Archives*
Parliamentary reports	– *Hansard*
Statistics for government departments	– *Monthly (and Annual) Digest of Statistics* – HMSO
World affairs, British and foreign embassies, Royal family, peerage, cabinet ministers, members of parliament, Bank of England, law courts, European Economic Community, United Nations	– *Whitaker's Almanack*
2 Office services	
Addressing envelopes	– See pp 11–12
Employment legislation	– *Croner's Reference Book for Employers* and other sources of reference on pp 77–82
Postal services (inland and overseas), National Girobank and Postal Order services, savings	– *Post Office Guide*
Printing terms and procedures	– *Authors' and Printers' Dictionary*
Safety	– See pp 126–7
Telegram, telex and telephone services (inland and overseas),	

Information	Source of reference
Confravision, Datel, Prestel	– *British Telecom Guide*
Telex subscribers	– *UK Telex Directory*

3 Organisations

Banks	– *Banker's Almanac and Year Book*
Building societies	– *Building Societies' Year Book*
Engineering	– *Kempe's Engineer's Year Book*
Insurance companies	– *Insurance Blue Book and Guide*
Names, addresses and telephone numbers	– Telephone directories
Newspapers, trade journals	– *Benn's Press Directory, Willings Press Guide*
Trade and professional associations, chambers of trade and commerce, trade unions	– *Directory of British Associations and Associations in Ireland*

4 People

Barristers and the judiciary	– *Bar List*
Biographies of living eminent people	– *Who's Who*
Biographies of people of international importance	– *International Year Book, Statesmen's Who's Who*
Clergymen of the Church of England	– *Crockford's Clerical Directory* (similar clerical directories are published for the other religious denominations)
Dentists	– *Dentists Register*
Directors and their joint stock companies	– *Directory of Directors*
Forms of address	– *Black's Titles and Forms of Address*
Medical practitioners	– *Medical Directory*
Names, addresses and telephone numbers	– Telephone directories
Nurses	– *Register of Nurses*
Peerage and baronetage	– *Debrett's Peerage and Baronetage*
Qualifications and addresses of professional bodies	– *British Qualifications*
Services personnel	– *Army List, Air Force List, Navy List*
Solicitors, courts, legal officers	– *Solicitors' Diary, Almanac and Legal Directory*

5 Secretarial services

Abbreviations and initials	– *Dictionary of Acronyms and Abbreviations*
Business equipment	– *Business Equipment Digest, Business Systems and Equipment, Office Equipment Index, Office Equipment News*
Forms of address	– *Black's Titles and Forms of Address*

	French, German, Spanish and Italian phrases	– Hamlyn pocket dictionaries and phrase books
	Shorthand outlines and meaning of words	– *Pitman's English and Shorthand Dictionary*
	Synonyms and antonyms	– *Roget's Thesaurus of English Words and Phrases*
	Typewriting terms and procedures	– *Pitman's Typewriting Dictionary*
6	**Trade**	
	Company data (industry and commerce)	– *UK Kompass*
	Companies (financial data, directors)	– *Stock Exchange Official Year Book*
	Manufacturers	– *Kelly's Directory of Manufacturers and Merchants*
	Names, addresses and telephone numbers	– Yellow pages (telephone directories)
	Prominent firms in the United Kingdom	– *Guide to British Enterprise*
7	**Travel**	
	Advice to businessmen travelling abroad	– *Hints to Businessmen* (Department of Trade and Industry)
	Air services	– *ABC World Airways Guide*
	Coach and bus services	– *ABC Coach and Bus Guide*
	Hotels and restaurants	– *ABC Hotel Guide, AA Members Handbook, Good Food Guide, Hotels and Restaurants in Great Britain, Financial Times World Hotel Directory, Michelin Guides*
	Location of places, names of towns, etc	– Gazetteer
	Motoring information (road maps, hotels, garages, distances between towns)	– *Automobile Association Members Handbook, Royal Automobile Club Guide and Handbook, AA and RAC Guides for motoring in Europe*
	Shipping services	– *ABC Shipping Guide, Lloyd's List and Shipping Gazette*
	Train times	– *ABC Railway Guide, British Rail timetables*
	Travel information (general)	– *Travel Trade Directory* and other sources of reference on pp 143–51, *ABC Guide to International Travel*

Interviewing

Senior secretaries are often asked to help interview staff for junior secretarial positions. The following is intended to help you in this and bring to your notice some of the more salient points involved in selecting staff.

An interview is a conversation between two or more people, face to face, to exchange information and views and assess attitudes, etc to achieve a defined objective, eg in the case of a job interview, to select the most suitable candidate.

To accomplish this with as much precision and reliability as possible it will be necessary to bring about free and uninhibited flow of conversation between the parties concerned.

Factors involved in creating these conditions:

1   Define the objectives of the interview by:
    a describing the job to be performed (job description – see below)
    b specifying the requirements of the job (job specification – see p 76)
2   Supply the candidates with all relevant information about the organisation, the job description and clear directions for locating the premises, preferably a location plan.
3   Prepare for the interviewer(s) full details of the candidates – obtained from the application forms and the results of any tests which have been set prior to the interview.
4   Arrange suitable accommodation for the interview which provides a quiet, private and relaxed atmosphere.
5   Allocate a comfortable waiting room for the candidates with cloakroom and refreshment facilities.
6   Arrange for the candidates to be shown round the premises to meet the staff and see the office where the successful candidate will work.
7   Allow sufficient time for each interview so that an accurate assessment can be made.

A **job description** should contain the following:
● job title
● job grading/salary scale
● purpose of the job and how it fits into the overall organisation, ie the name of the department, the immediate superior to whom the person reports, any staff who report to the person and those with whom the person liaises
● a detailed description of the duties and responsibilities involved in the job

A **job specification** describes the sort of person required to do the job, including:
- physical attributes, eg age, voice, sight etc
- attainments, eg qualifications and previous experience
- general intelligence
- special aptitudes, eg secretarial skills
- interests
- disposition
- special circumstances

Techniques of interviewing

A successful interviewer:

1 Studies the candidates' papers; knows the qualities and skills needed to fill the vacancy (from a job description/ specification); and plans the approach to be used at the interview in order to achieve the objectives.
2 Is pleasant and has the ability to establish an early rapport and put the candidates at ease so that they communicate freely.
3 Asks questions clearly and concisely, allowing the candidate to do most of the talking; listens carefully to what is said and notes what is not said.
4 Asks questions which encourage the candidate to demonstrate not only her knowledge and experience, but her attitude, manner and motivation. Questions which can be answered simply by 'yes' or 'no' rarely contribute much to the interview.
5 Asks extra questions to discover the depth of knowledge and information which might otherwise be withheld if not questioned.
6 Does not make a judgment until a candidate has had a full hearing and all relevant facts have been established.
7 Avoids excessive note-taking during the interview. Brief, unobtrusive notes can normally be made without it being obvious to the candidate that everything spoken is being recorded. More detailed note-taking should follow immediately after the candidate has left the room and, at this stage, an interview merit grading form can be completed to provide a score of the candidate's performance.
8 Gives the candidate the chance to ask questions about the organisation or the vacancy.
9 Knows when sufficient information has been obtained for the interview to be ended.

An interview merit grading form, designed to place the candidates in the order of acceptability, may include some or all of the following:

- results from a pre-interview test
- qualifications – general education
- qualifications – business and secretarial
- relevant business experience
- general appearance
- health record
- ability to communicate
- integrity/reliability/adaptability
- initiative
- personality, including the ability to relate to others
- energy/stability
- attitude/motivation
- organising ability
- quality of interests, hobbies etc

Each item is graded on a five-point scale

Itineraries

See Travel arrangements p 146.

Legislation relating to office practice and employment

The following Acts of Parliament, which have been introduced in recent years, contain important provisions for employees and for those who are responsible for the employment of staff and the administration of office work:

Equal Pay Act 1970
Health and Safety at Work Act 1974 (incorporating the provisions of the Offices, Shops and Railway Premises Act 1963)
Sex Discrimination Act 1975
Race Relations Act 1976
Employment Protection (Consolidation) Act 1978

Equal Pay Act 1970

The aim of this Act is to prevent discrimination between men and women concerning their terms and conditions of employment. Employers are required to give equal pay where men and women are employed on the same or broadly similar work. Any disputes arising under the Act can be referred to an industrial tribunal.

Further information: *Equal Pay – A Guide to the Equal Pay Act 1970* (HMSO)

Health and Safety at Work etc Act 1974

The health and safety of office employees is protected by this Act. It is additional to other health and safety at work legislation, such as the Offices, Shops and Railway Premises Act of 1963. The greater part of that Act and subsidiary regulations remain current, but revision and updating will be made as necessary in the future.

The aim of the Health and Safety at Work etc Act is to:

a secure the health, safety and welfare of people at work

b protect people other than those at work against risks to health or safety arising out of or in connection with the activities of persons at work

c control the keeping and use of explosive or highly flammable or otherwise dangerous substances, and generally preventing the unlawful acquisition, possession and use of such substances

d control the emission into the atmosphere of noxious or offensive substances from premises

One of the principal objectives of the Act is to involve everybody at the workplace – both management and employees – and to create an awareness of the importance of achieving high standards of health and safety.

Duties of the employer The employer must provide his employees with:

1 Safe place of work with safe access and exit.
2 Safe equipment (including efficient maintenance).
3 Safe systems of work.
4 Safe working environment and adequate facilities and arrangements for their welfare.
5 Safe methods for handling, storing and transporting goods.
6 Instruction, training and supervision of safe practices.
7 Consultation with a view to making and maintaining effective arrangements for promoting health and safety.
8 Where appropriate, a written statement on health and safety and the means of carrying out that policy.

It is also the employer's duty to protect persons not in his employment, eg the public, customers, visiting workers, delivery men, etc, when they are on the premises.

Duties of employees It is the duty of every employee while at work to:

1 Take reasonable care for the health and safety of himself and of other persons who may be affected by his acts or omissions at work.
2 Cooperate with his employer, supervisor or any other persons to enable them to fulfil their obligations.
3 Refrain from misusing or interfering with anything provided for the health and safety of themselves or others.

Safety precautions extend beyond the office as office employees are sometimes required to visit other parts of the organisation, such as warehouses, workshops and stores, and are then subject to the dangers entailed in the operation of, for instance, fork lift trucks and cranes and the movement of heavy goods. The fact that office staff are infrequent visitors to these workplaces can easily add to the risks of injury unless they are especially careful and conscious of the dangers.

Offices, Shops and Railway Premises Act 1963

The performance of clerical work suffers if the physical conditions are below standard. The provisions contained in this Act are, therefore, very important for efficient office administration.

After providing that all premises must be kept clean, with floors cleaned at least once weekly, the Act deals with overcrowding. There must be not less than 3.715 sq m (40 sq ft) of floor space for each worker – inclusive of furniture and equipment. A reasonable temperature must be provided and maintained in all rooms in which employees work otherwise than for short periods. A temperature will not be regarded as reasonable if it falls below 16°C (60.8°F) after the first hour of work.

Suitable and sufficient lighting must be provided. No specific standard is stated regarding the intensity of the light, but later regulations may do this (20–30 lumens are normally regarded as satisfactory). Adequate supplies of either fresh air or artificially purified air must be circulated to secure the ventilation of offices.

Premises must have suitable conveniences and washing facilities at places conveniently accessible to all employees. Running hot and cold water must be supplied, together with soap and clean towels. Drinking water must be available and also suitable places to hang up clothing and facilities for drying them. First-aid boxes must be provided in all premises so as to be readily accessible. Safety measures and fire precautions are also included in the Act. Seats provided for workers who normally perform their work sitting must be suitable in design, construction and dimensions for the worker and for the kind of work done.

Further information: Health and Safety at Work – Basic Rules for Safety and Health at Work (HMSO)

Sex Discrimination Act 1975

This Act aims to make sex discrimination unlawful in employment (including opportunities for promotion); training and education; the provision of goods, facilities and services and in the disposal and management of premises. The Equal Opportunities Commission enforces the Act and seeks to promote equality of opportunity between the sexes.

Further information: Leaflets supplied by the Equal Opportunities Commission:

Equal Opportunities: A Guide for Employers
Equal Opportunities: A Guide for Employees
Equal Opportunities: A Short Guide to the Sex Discrimination Act 1975
Equal Opportunities: Education
Equal Opportunities: Housing, Goods, Facilities and Services

Leaflet supplied by HMSO:

Sex Discrimination – A Guide to the Sex Discrimination Act 1975

Race Relations Act 1976

This Act makes it unlawful to discriminate by race, colour etc in the employment of staff (including recruitment, terms of employment, promotion and dismissal); education, public services and housing; membership of trade unions and professional bodies and in advertisements. The Commission for Racial Equality enforces the Act and seeks to promote good race relations.

Further information: Publications from the Commission for Racial Equality:

Equal Opportunity in Employment: A Guide for Employers
A Guide to the New Race Relations Act: Advertising
A Guide to the New Race Relations Act: Employment
A Guide to the New Race Relations Act: Landlords and Accommodation Agencies

Employment Protection (Consolidation) Act 1978

This Act deals with various individual rights of people at work. The major provisions are as follows:

Contracts of employment Employees working for 16 hours or more a week must, not later than 13 weeks after beginning work, be given a written statement or contract of employment containing: the names of the parties to the contract; date of commencement; whether employment with a previous employer counts as part of the employee's period of continuous employment and, if it does, the relevant dates; rate of pay; normal working hours; holiday entitlement; rules relating to sickness/injury absence and sick pay; pension scheme; length of notice employee is entitled to receive and give; job title; disciplinary rules and the person the employee can consult if dissatisfied with a disciplinary decision; the person to whom the employee can take a job grievance.

Notice to terminate employment The notice required by an employer to terminate a contract of employment of an employee who has been continuously employed for at least 4 weeks is:

- not less than one week's notice if employment has been continuous for less than 2 years
- not less than one week's notice for each year of continuous employment if employment has been continuous for 2 years or more but less than 12 years
- not less than 12 week's notice if employment has been continuous for 12 years or more.

An employee must give the employer at least one week's notice if employment has been continuous for 4 weeks or more and this period does not increase with longer employment.

Dismissal procedures An employee who has been continuously employed (ie 16 hours or more per week) for 52 weeks or more (or has been employed for 8 hours or more, but less than 16 hours per week, for 5 years or more) has the right not to be unfairly dismissed by an employer. If dismissed, the employee is entitled to take the matter up with an industrial tribunal.

An employee who has worked for at least 26 weeks continuously is entitled to a written statement giving details of the reason for dismissal if a contract is terminated, or a contract is terminated without notice by the employer.

Pay statements An employer must give employees on or before pay day detailed pay statements containing: gross pay; fixed deductions and the purposes for which they are made; variable deductions and the purposes for which they are made; net pay; where the pay is paid in different ways, the amount and method of payment of each part-payment.

Guarantee payments Employees who have been employed continuously for at least 4 weeks are entitled to a guarantee payment of wages when there is no work to do because of a reduced demand for the employer's business or any other occurrence affecting the work which the employee is engaged to do.

Medical suspension An employee who has been employed continuously for 4 weeks or more is entitled to be paid if suspended on medical grounds. The employee is entitled to receive a normal week's pay for every week of suspension up to a maximum of 26 weeks.

Maternity provisions Employees are entitled to receive maternity pay and to be granted maternity leave provided they have:

- been employed continuously with the employer for at least 2 years by the eleventh week before the expected confinement date
- a contract of employment
- informed the employer that they are leaving (normally in writing)
- in the event of wishing to return, informed their employer in writing that they will be absent because of pregnancy and that they intend to return to work, giving the expected date of confinement

Time off work

1 Employers must allow their employees who are officials of recognised independent trade unions time off work with pay to undertake industrial relations duties and appropriate training for these duties. Members of independent trade unions recognised by employers must also be given reasonable time off during working hours without pay to take part in union activities.

2 Employees who are magistrates, members of local government authorities, governors of schools, etc must be allowed reasonable time off work, without pay, to perform their duties.

3 Employees with at least 2 years of continuous employment who are made redundant must be given reasonable time off work to arrange training or a new job.

Further information: A useful source of reference on all aspects of employment law is *Croner's Reference Book for Employers*. A monthly amendment service is provided in order to keep the information up-to-date.

Licences

Applying for, or renewing, licences is frequently a task which the secretary is expected to do. The renewal dates can be remembered by entering them in your diary or in a follow-up system (see pp 38–40).

Licence	Address for renewal

Broadcast receiving
  Black and white
  Colour
	– Post offices or National
	  Television Licence Records
	  Office, Bristol BS98 1TL

Business reply postal packets Franking machine Freepost Postage Forward parcel	– The Head Postmaster of your district
Dog Game	– Post offices

Motor vehicles
  Driving licences
	– Driver and Vehicle Licensing
	  Centre, Swansea SA99 1AB
	  (application forms obtainable
	  from post offices)

Heavy goods vehicle driving
  licences
	– Traffic Area Offices of
	  Department of Transport

Taxation	– Local Vehicle Licensing Office or post offices

Mail – incoming and outgoing

Post Office services for mailroom procedures

Collection of mail by the Post Office The Post Office will collect mail from an office provided the following quantities are being despatched:

a 1st and 2nd class letters, when there are at least 1000 or the total postage is £100 or more

b special collections of parcels where the number at any one time is at least 100

c a regular collection of parcels if there are at least 20 at a time

Private box A box, rented at the Post Office, for the collection of mail.

Private bag A lockable bag used for collecting and delivering mail.

Franking machines See p 84.

Franking of mail by the Post Office Mail can be franked 'paid' by the Post Office when there are at least 120 packets (or 20 parcels). The printed postage impression service in which 'Postage Paid' is printed or stamped on mail can be used if there are at least 5000 letters or 100 parcels.

Full details of all services: *Post Office Guide*

Mailing equipment

Addressing machine	– addressing envelopes, etc; see also p 97
Collating machine	– sorting and collating of documents
Date and time stamp	– stamping the date and time on incoming mail
Folding machine	– automatic folding of documents
Franking machine	– printing postal impressions on mail. Machines must be leased or purchased from the supplying companies authorised by the Post Office: Hasler (Great Britain) Ltd, Hasler Works, Commerce Way, Croydon CR0 4XA; Pitney Bowes PLC, The Pinnacles, Harlow, Essex CM19 5BD; Roneo Vickers Ltd, Mailroom Division, PO Box 66, South Street, Romford RM1 2AR
Inserting and mailing machine	– mechanises the following procedures: collating; opening envelope flap; sealing envelope; franking postage impression; counting number of items and stacking envelopes
Jogger	– Vibrating papers into alignment ready for stapling or binding
Letter opening machine	– slitting envelopes received in the mail
Package tying machine	– tying string/tape round parcels
Rolling and wrapping machine	– preparing newspapers, magazines etc for posting
Sealing machine	– moistening and sealing flaps of envelopes
Shredder	– shredding documents

Sponge/roller moistener	– moistening stamps and envelopes
Stapler	– fixing wire staples into documents
Tucking and folding machine	– preparing documents for posting without envelopes
Weighing machine	– weighing packets for calculation of postage

Mailing equipment suppliers

Bell & Howell Ltd, 33–35 Woodthorpe Road, Ashford, Middx TW15 2RJ

Envopak Group Sales Ltd, Powerscroft Road, Sidcup, Kent DA14 5EF

Hasler (Great Britain) Ltd, Commerce Way, Croydon, Surrey CR0 4XA

Mailing & Mechanisation Ltd, 83 Copers Cope Road, Beckenham, Kent BR3 1NR

Pitney Bowes PLC, The Pinnacles, Elizabeth Way, Harlow, Essex CM19 5BD

Roneo Alcatel Ltd, PO Box 3, South Street, Romford, Essex RM1 2AR

Meetings

Documents

Agenda A programme of business to be discussed at a meeting, usually incorporating the notice convening the meeting. Sources for the agenda:
- previous agenda (recurring items)
- previous minutes (continuing items)
- constitution (constitutional items)
- chairman and members may request items to be included

An agenda is sent out 7 to 14 days before the meeting so that the participants can consider the matters to be discussed.

Attendance sheet Record of people present at a meeting. Usually members sign the attendance sheet as they enter the room.

Chairman's agenda This contains more information than the ordinary agenda, and spaces are left on the right-hand side of the paper for the chairman to make his own notes. The additional

```
STAFF WELFARE COMMITTEE


A meeting of the Staff Welfare Committee will be held
in the Boardroom on Friday 14 October 19-- at 1530 hrs.



AGENDA


1  Apologies for absence.

2  Minutes of the last meeting.

3  Matters arising from the minutes.

4  Staff canteen: To receive a report from the Canteen   Paper 1
   Manager concerning proposed increases in prices.       attached

5  Car park: To consider the working party report on a    Paper 2
   new layout for the car park.                           to follow

6  To receive proposals for the staff Christmas Dinner.

7  Any other business.

8  Date of next meeting.

K ABRAHAM

Secretary
```

A specimen agenda

information provides the chairman with details necessary for the efficient conduct of the meeting.

Minutes A record of the proceedings of a meeting. The key factors concerning the taking of minutes:

1 Record the exact wording of resolutions passed or decisions reached with the names of the proposers and seconders.
2 Note the main arguments for and against the decisions.
3 Write the minutes as soon as possible after the meeting while the discussions are fresh in the mind.
4 Write minutes wholly in the third person and in the past tense.
5 Be as brief as possible as a summary is required – not a verbatim record.

```
MINUTES OF MEETING      A meeting of the Staff Welfare Committee was held
                        in the Boardroom on Friday 14 October 19-- at 1530 hrs.


                        Present:

                        Miss C Parsons (in the Chair)
                        Mr P L Brown
                        Mrs J Clarke
                        Miss C H Ellis
                        Mr T R Moon
                        Mr G Strong
                        Miss K Abraham (Secretary)
                        Mr F Morris (Canteen Manager)

Apologies               Apologies were received on behalf of Miss J Tucker
                        and Mr V Williams.

Minutes                 The minutes of the last meeting, which had been
                        circulated, were taken as read and approved and were
                        signed by the Chairman.

Matters arising         There were no matters arising out of the minutes.

Staff canteen           The Canteen Manager submitted a report outlining the
                        current financial position of the canteen. Since
                        October of last year, when the price of meals was last
                        increased, food costs had risen by 20% and he
                        proposed a similar increase in the price of meals in
                        order to meet the extra costs. It was generally felt
                        that, at a time when salary increases were less than
                        10%, an increase of 20% for canteen meals would be
                        unacceptable. Miss Ellis suggested offering a smaller
                        choice of meals as a possible means of reducing costs.
                        Mr Strong was of the opinion that the firm's subsidy
                        should be increased to meet the higher costs.
                        After much discussion it was agreed to defer increasing
                        prices until the Chairman and the Canteen Manager have
                        had a meeting with the Personnel Manager to seek an
                        increase in the meals subsidy, and the Canteen Manager
                        has considered other means of saving expenditure such
                        as reducing the choice of meals offered.

Any other business      Miss Parsons stated that the London office
                        had adopted flexitime and she considered that
                        the majority of staff at this branch would
                        like to change over to it. Members agreed to
                        seek the views of staff and to report back
                        their findings to the next meeting.

Date of next meeting    It was decided to hold the next meeting of the
                        Committee on Tuesday 7 November 19--.



                        Chairman

                        7 November 19--
```

An example of minutes

6 Write clearly so that there is no possible doubt about the
decisions reached.

7 Arrange the items in the same order as on the agenda.

8 Prepare a draft for approval by the chairman before typing
the final copy.

Reports of meeting: See p 125

Glossary of meeting terms

Ad hoc 'Arranged for this purpose'. An *ad hoc* sub-committee is appointed to carry out one particular piece of work, such as the arrangements for the visit of a very important person (VIP). These committees are sometimes called special or special-purpose committees.

Addendum An amendment which adds words to a motion.

Addressing the chair A member wishing to speak on a point must rise and address the Chair in the following way:

Mr Chairman – for a gentleman.

Madam Chairman – for a lady.

All remarks must be addressed to the chairman, and members must not discuss matters between themselves at a meeting.

Adjournment Subject to the articles, rules or constitution of an organisation, the chairman, with the consent of the members of the meeting, may adjourn it in order to postpone further discussion, or because of the shortage of time. Adequate notice of an adjourned meeting must be given.

Amendment A proposal to alter a motion by adding or deleting words. It must be proposed, seconded and put to the meeting in the customary way.

Casting vote A second vote usually allowed to the chairman, except in the case of a company meeting. A casting vote is used only when there is an equal number of votes 'for' and 'against' a motion.

Closure A motion submitted with the object of ending the discussion on a matter before the meeting.

Cooption The power given to a committee to allow others to serve on the committee. A cooption must be the result of a majority vote of the existing members of the organisation.

Disturbance A person causing a disturbance at a meeting may be ejected with or without the aid of the police provided that the meeting has not been announced as 'public'.

Dropped motion A motion that has to be dropped either because there is no seconder or because the meeting want it to be abandoned.

En bloc The voting of, say, a committee *en bloc*, that is, electing or re-electing all members of a committee by the passing of one resolution.

Ex officio 'By virtue of office'. A person may be a member of a committee by virtue of his office; or the holding of one office may automatically be a qualification for the holding of another.

Going into committee A motion 'that the meeting go into committee' is moved if less restricted discussion is thought necessary. A motion 'that the meeting be resumed' gives the meeting authority to proceed at the point where it left off.

In camera A meeting which is not open to the public.

Intra vires Within the power of the person or body concerned.

Kangaroo closure The chairman of a committee can jump from one amendment to another omitting those he considers to be less important or repetitive.

Lie on the table A letter or document is said to 'lie on the table' when it is decided at a meeting to take no action upon the business in it.

Majority The articles and rules of the organisation will state the majority of votes needed to carry a motion.

Memorandum and articles of association Regulations drawn up by a company setting out the objects for which the company is formed and defining the manner in which its business shall be conducted.

Motion A motion must normally be written and handed to the chairman or secretary before the meeting. The mover of the motion speaks on it and has the right to reply at the close of the discussion. The seconder may then speak to the motion only once. If there is no seconder, a motion is dropped and cannot be introduced again. When put to a meeting, the motion becomes 'the question' or 'the proposal', and when it is passed, it is called 'the resolution'. A motion on something which has not been included on the agenda can be moved only if 'leave of urgency' has been agreed by the meeting or it has been included under the customary item 'any other business'.

Nem Con 'No one contradicting', ie, there are no votes against the motion, but some members have not voted at all.

Next business A motion 'that the meeting proceed with next business' is a method of delaying the decision on any matter brought before the meeting.

No confidence When the members of a meeting disagree with the chairman they may pass a vote of 'no confidence' in the chair. When this happens the chairman must vacate the chair in favour of his deputy or some other person nominated by the meeting. There must be a substantial majority of members in favour of this decision.

Point of order This is a question regarding the procedure at a meeting or a query relating to the standing orders or constitution raised by a member during the course of the meeting, eg, absence of quorum.

Poll Term for the method of voting at an election, usually a secret vote by ballot paper. The way in which a poll is to be conducted is generally laid down in the standing orders or constitution of the organisation.

Postponement The action taken to defer a meeting to a later date.

Proxy One acting for another, or a document authorising a person to attend a meeting and vote on behalf of another person.

Putting the question To conclude the discussion on a motion it is customary for the chairman to 'put the question' by announcing 'The question before the meeting is . . .'

Question be now put When members feel that sufficient discussion has taken place on a motion, it may be moved 'that the question be now put'. If this is carried, only the proposer of the motion may speak and then a vote is taken. If the motion 'question be now put' is defeated, discussion may be continued.

Quorum The minimum number of persons who must be in attendance to constitute a meeting. This is stated in the constitution or rules of the organisation.

Reference back An amendment referring a report or other item of business back for further consideration to the body or person submitting it. If the motion 'reference back' is defeated, the discussion is continued.

Resolution A formal decision carried at a meeting. It must be proposed, seconded and put to the meeting in the customary way. A resolution cannot be rescinded at the meeting at which it is adopted.

Rider An additional clause or sentence added to a resolution after it has been passed. It differs from an amendment in that it adds to a resolution instead of altering it. A rider has to be proposed, seconded and put to the meeting in the same way as a motion.

Right of reply The proposer of a resolution has the right of reply when the resolution has been fully discussed. He is allowed to reply only once, and afterwards the motion is put to the meeting.

Scrutineer Person who counts and closely examines the votes at an election.

Seating arrangements It is customary for the chairman to be seated at the head of the table with the secretary on his right and the treasurer on his left.

Sine die Without an appointed day, or indefinitely.

Standing orders Rules compiled by the organisation regulating the manner in which its business is to be conducted. It may also have the title 'Constitution'.

Status quo Used to refer to a matter in which there is to be no change.

Sub-committee A sub-committee may be appointed by a committee to deal with some specific branch of its work. It must carry out such functions as are delegated to it by the committee and must report to the committee periodically.

Teller Title given to the person appointed to count the votes at a meeting.

Ultra vires Beyond the legal power or authority of a company or organisation.

Unanimous When all members of a meeting have voted in favour of a resolution it is said to be carried 'unanimously'.

Meetings – the secretary's role

Before the meeting	*On the day of the meeting*	*After the meeting*
1 Book a suitable room	**1** Attend early, bringing with you the items referred to in **5** of the previous column	**1** Clear the room of all papers
2 Prepare the agenda in consultation with the chairman and distribute it to members	**2** Arrange for direction signs to the committee room to be displayed	**2** Ensure that all documents are returned to the office
3 Prepare a chairman's agenda	**3** Ensure that the seating arrangements are in order	**3** Prepare draft minutes for approval by the chairman
4 Obtain any necessary statements or documents from members who cannot be present but who are known to have strong views on items to be discussed	**4** See that each member has a supply of writing paper	**4** When approved, type the minutes in final form for distribution to members
5 Collect together the following items required for the meeting:	**5** Provide water and glasses, order refreshments and arrange ash-trays in convenient positions	**5** Type any correspondence resulting from the meeting
a stationery, including writing paper and shorthand note book	**6** Check that members sign the attendance register	**6** File any papers used at the meeting, as well as copies of correspondence typed in **5**
b spare copies of the agenda	**7** Read the minutes of the last meeting, if these have not been circulated; letters of apology and any other correspondence	**7** If the chairman is also your employer see that the date of the next meeting is entered in his diary and yours
c minutes of the previous meeting	**8** Assist the chairman in supplying information from files as required during the meeting	
d all relevant papers and files of the correspondence, including letters of apology received from members unable to attend	**9** Record the details of the decisions reached, noting who proposed and who seconded motions as well as the results of the voting	
e attendance register or sheet		
f any books of reference, standing orders, etc		

Methods of payment

Name	Issued by	Description
Bill of exchange	Bank	Commonly used as payment for exports – may be accompanied by shipping documents giving title to goods
Cash	–	Frequently used for payment 'on the spot' eg petty cash transactions. When sent through the post, cash must be registered in a special registered envelope supplied by the Post Office
Cash on Delivery	Post Office	Up to £300 can be collected by a postman on delivery of a parcel, compensation fee parcel or registered letter and remitted to the sender by special order
Cheque	Bank	See p 15 for advice to bank account holders
	Post Office (Girobank)	Cheques used by girobank account holders. Payment is not effected until the cheque has been cleared at the Girobank Centre
Credit card	Bank American Express Diners Club	eg Barclay or Access for purchasing goods or services on credit
Credit transfer (or bank giro)	Bank	Making payments through a bank without having to send cheques by post, credit being transferred from the drawer's bank to the payee's bank
	Post Office	National Giro – using a transfer form for making payments through the Girobank Centre
Direct debit	Bank	System for arranging periodic payments, the

		payee requesting the bank to collect them from the drawer's account
Documentary letter of credit	Bank	Written undertaking by a bank to an exporter to pay within a specified period of time for goods or services on presentation of documentary evidence
Draft	Bank	A draft is drawn up by a bank in favour of a creditor in settlement of an amount owing, normally payable on demand. It is used for paying large sums where an ordinary cheque may not be acceptable, eg when buying a car or house
	Post Office (Girobank)	Similar to the above except that it is drawn up by the Girobank
Express international money transfer	Bank	Telex or cable is used to instruct an overseas bank to pay an exporter
International money transfer	Bank	An importer's bank instructs an overseas bank by airmail to pay an exporter
Letter of credit	Bank	See Documentary letter of credit (above)
Overseas postal and payment orders	Post Office	Issued to many foreign countries for payment in the currency of the country concerned. Further details in the *Post Office Guide*
Postal order	Post Office	Issued in various amounts up to £10. Can be crossed to ensure that payment is made only through a bank
Promissory note	Bank	Issued on behalf of buyer who promises to pay the seller a sum of money at a specified time
Standing order	Bank	An order to a bank to pay a person or business a certain sum of money periodically from a customer's account.
	Post Office (Girobank)	Similar to the above except that the order is placed with the Girobank

Name	Issued by	Description
Telegraphic payment order	Post Office	Telegraph is used for transmitting sums up to the value of £100. Useful when urgent payment has to be made
Trans cash	Post Office (Girobank)	Credit transfer system where the remitter deposits the cash for payment at a Post Office

Microfilming

Filming documents in a reduced size for storage and integration with the computer and word processor for information handling. The main advantage of microfilming is space-saving, eg 25 000 documents can be stored in one 4 in by 4 in by 1 in film cartridge.

Glossary of terms

Acetate jacket 'Loose-leaf' system for holding strips of microfilm in horizontal grooves – useful for periodic updating.

Aperture card An 80-column punched card with a microfilm mounted on it. The punched holes denote the contents. Reference numbers are used for quick sorting and retrieval of the card when it is required for viewing or for reproducing paper copies.

Camera Equipment for filming documents.

CAR Computer-assisted retrieval, a system which has a built-in microprocessor which interrogates the computer and retrieves the required microfilm. A reference number is keyed into a terminal and relevant information from the computer index is displayed on a VDU indicating the film magazine where the microfilm is stored. The desired documents are then automatically displayed on the reader/printer and a hard copy made, if required.

Cartridge Container which holds microfilm and makes it easier to handle because there is no lacing of the film, no rewinding and the film is protected.

CIM Computer input microfilm, a system which uses a camera to film documents for subsequent optical character recognition input into a computer.

COM Computer output on microfilm or computer-originated microfilm. Data from a computer is recorded directly on to roll film or microfiche. When documents are required for reference they are either viewed on a reader or a hard copy is produced using a reader/printer.

Duplicator Equipment for reproducing copies of microfiche.

Edge-punched cards Edge-punched cards with microfilms mounted for ease of sorting and selecting documents.

Micro-comparator Equipment for viewing and comparing two microfiches.

Microfiche Sheet of microfilm with rows of images. Appropriate for quick reference to a large number of related documents which do not require periodic updating.

Processor Equipment for developing and processing film.

Reader/printer Equipment for viewing film and printing copies.

Roll film Continuous roll of film used for sequentially filed documents where no insertions are required.

Microfilm applications

1 Cheap transportation of documents, especially when sent by airmail.
2 Security of valuable documents, eg legal documents can be stored in more than one place.
3 Engineering drawings.
4 Systems such as sales invoicing, copy orders, cheque payments.
5 Parts manuals.
6 Journals and newspapers for reference in libraries.

Key factors when considering the use of microfilm:

1 The volume and nature of records which must be kept for reference and the office space available for storing them.
2 The frequency of reference to the records and the need for speedy retrieval.
3 The importance of security and durability of records.
4 The need for standardising the storage and retrieval of documents.
5 The cost of the necessary microfilming equipment set against savings in filing cabinets, copy papers and files.
6 The need for microfilming equipment to be compatible with existing equipment and procedures.
7 The type of microfilm to be used, eg jacket, cartridge, roll film, aperture card and microfiche (see above for an explanation of their uses).

8 The type of installation, eg:

    a all operations performed in-house by a camera, reader/ printer and processing unit

    b use of equipment which links microfilming with computer or word processor

    c having a camera and reader and arranging for the films to be processed by a bureau

    d having reading equipment only and using a bureau to film and process the records

The type of installation selected will normally be determined by the number of records filmed (*a* for a large amount) and the availability of computing and word processing equipment (*b*). If the records were confidential *c* and *d* would not be suitable.

An intelligent microimage terminal for retrieving and viewing microfilm

Suppliers of microfilm equipment and accessories

Agfa Gavaert Ltd, 27 Great West Road, Brentford, Middx TW8 9AX

Bell & Howell Ltd, 33–35 Woodthorpe Road, Ashford, Middx TW15 2RJ

Finlay Microfilm Co Ltd, Finlay House, PO Box 68, 18 Woodside Road, Amersham, Bucks HP7 0BH

Imtec Microfilm Ltd, Southfield Road Trading Estate, Nailsea, Bristol BS19 1JE

Kodak Ltd, PO Box 66, Kodak House, Station Road, Hemel Hempstead HP1 1JU

Ozalid (UK) Ltd, Topasol House, Langston Road, Loughton, Essex IG10 3TH

Office equipment

When selecting a new item of equipment, consider the following questions:

1 Is it necessary? Will it produce better quality work and what are its advantages over existing methods?
2 Will the equipment serve its purpose for future needs, say four or five years?
3 Is it appropriate for your use? Would it be suitable for other uses and what size do you need?
4 Would it be compatible with equipment already in use?
5 What is the price of the equipment, installation, maintenance, software and stationery?
6 What is the cheapest method of purchase: outright purchase, hire purchase, leasing or renting? How soon will it become obsolete?
7 Consider the manufacturer's reputation: Is the firm reliable and is there a good after-sales service? Have other local firms bought it?
8 What is involved in training existing staff to operate the equipment? Will new staff have to be employed and, if so, are they available locally?
9 Are there any special requirements to house the equipment and store materials?
10 Will there be a noise/ventilation problem?
11 What will the effect be on staff morale? Have staff/unions been consulted?
12 What will its effects be on customers?

Addressing machines

Equipment used to reproduce information from stencil cards, plates, discs etc on to envelopes, labels and forms.

Types of addressing machine
Stencil
Spirit
Metal and plastic plate

Foil master
Electronic (microprocessor)

Applications
Addressing envelopes/labels/cards
Entering descriptions on stock cards
Imprinting clock cards, pay envelopes and fixed data on pay record sheets
Addressing advertising literature
Entering details of customers on ledger sheets, index cards and files
Addressing monthly statements and invoices

An addressing machine

Suppliers of addressing machines
Addressing Systems International Ltd, Rosedale Road, Richmond, Surrey TW9 2SZ
AM International Information Systems Ltd, PO Box 17, Maylands Avenue, Hemel Hempstead, Herts HP2 7ET
Pitney Bowes PLC, The Pinnacles, Elizabeth Way, Harlow, Essex CM19 5BD
Renaddress Ltd, 263 The Vale, London W3 7QA
Roneo Alcatel Ltd, PO Box 3, South Street, Romford, Essex RM1 2AR
Scriptomatic Ltd, Scriptomatic House, Torrington Park, London N12 9SU

Calculators

Electronic calculators with printing facilities are commonly used in offices for tasks which involve calculations. The tally roll is useful for providing printed proof of the accuracy of calculations and also for attaching to documents for future reference and checking. Calculators can be used for addition, subtraction, multiplication, division, percentages and square roots. Functions include:

- a decimal point selector (including a floating decimal point)
- sub-total key
- rounding switch which rounds up or down when the fixed decimal point is chosen in multiplication and division
- item counter switch providing the total number of items added or subtracted
- non-add key for printing reference numbers which are not to be included in the calculation
- automatic constant feature which enables you to add, subtract, multiply or divide by the same number repeatedly without having to re-enter the number for each new calculation
- memory to provide for the storage of products or quotients during the course of a calculation

Applications
Calculating and checking time cards and pay roll totals
Invoice extensions
Stock valuations
Foreign exchange rates
Bills of quantities
Sales analysis

An electronic calculator

Suppliers of calculators

British Olivetti Ltd, 30 Berkeley Square, London W1X 6AG
Burroughs Machines Ltd, Heathrow House, Bath Road, Hounslow, Middx TW5 9QL

Facit-Addo Ltd, Maidstone Road, Rochester, Kent ME1 3QN
Office International (Group) Ltd, International House, Windmill Road, Sunbury-on-Thames, Middx TW16 7HR
Olympia Business Machines Ltd, 203–205 Old Marylebone Road, London NW1 5QS
Sharp Electronics (UK) Ltd, Sharp House, Thorp Road, Manchester M10 9BE

Copiers

Electrostatic copiers are in general use today and can be divided into three main categories: high-speed plain paper copiers; low to medium-speed plain paper copiers; and coated paper copiers.

Plain paper copiers (indirect process) An image of the document is projected on to a light-sensitive surface, a selenium-coated drum or plate, which is electronically charged. Where the original is dark there is a charge and where it is light there is no charge. Powdered ink is attracted to the charged 'dark' areas. Plain 'bond-type' paper is brought into contact with the drum or plate and an electrical charge beneath the paper attracts the powder from drum or plate to paper, forming a positive image. The powder is fused to the paper by heat to form a permanent copy. Machines are available with suitable paper-handling devices for use as copier/duplicators to produce larger quantities.

Coated paper copiers (direct process) The image is reflected directly on to sensitised paper coated with zinc oxide (a photo-conductor). The light induces an electrostatic charge on the paper which attracts particles of black toner powder in liquid form. The toner sticks to the image areas where the charge has built up and it is fused permanently and dried by heat and/or pressure.

Electrostatic copiers can have a high degree of automatic control with warning lights to draw the operator's attention when, for example, the paper or toner is running out, or the paper is mis-feeding.

Multi-station collating devices are available for rapid collating and stapling of copies for booklets, etc. There are various ways of feeding the paper into these copiers, but the main ones are: cartridges and cassettes; suction from stacks of paper and continuous rolls fed and cut as required.

Applications
Reproducing copies of: printed documents, legal documents, insurance policies, statistical returns, diagrams and drawings, extracts from books and magazines, incoming letters required for several departments
Making overhead transparencies
Preparing offset litho masters

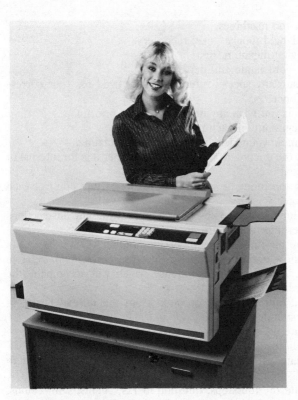

A plain paper copier

Suppliers of copiers

A B Dick Ltd, PO Box 24, 88–95 High Street, Brentford, Middx TW8 8BA

3M United Kingdom PLC, 3M House, PO Box 1, Bracknell, Berks RG12 1JU

Office International (Group) Ltd, International House, Windmill Road, Sunbury-on-Thames, Middx TW16 7HR

Ozalid (UK) Ltd, Topasol House, Langston Road, Loughton, Essex IG10 3TH

Rank Xerox (UK) Ltd, Bridge House, Oxford Road, Uxbridge, Middx UB8 1HS

Roneo Alcatel Ltd, PO Box 3, South Street, Romford, Essex RM1 2AR

Dictation equipment

There are three main categories of dictation equipment:

1 Central dictation network systems used by large organisations. This system can be connected to a PABX or PAX telephone system or it can be a separately wired circuit.

2 Desk-top machines.
3 Hand-held (pocket-size) recorders.

When giving dictation, first:
1 State your name and department.
2 Indicate any special reference to be used for your correspondence.
3 State if you wish any item to be given priority.

At the beginning of each passage:
1 Assemble your facts before you start dictating.
2 State the document required and whether it is for internal or external use.
3 Mark the index or scale to show the starting point of each passage.
4 Say how many copies you require with any instructions concerning their distribution.
5 Quote the reference number/file number.
6 Dictate names and addresses of correspondents or refer to their names in correspondence which will accompany the recording.
7 Say if you require a variation from the normal layout of correspondence.
8 Dictate the salutation.

During the course of dictation:
1 Indicate paragraphing and capital letters *before* the text to which the instruction refers.
2 Dictate the full stops, question marks, colons, semi-colons, dashes, exclamation marks, brackets and quotation marks. You are not expected to dictate every comma, but you can assist the typist by the inflections of your voice. It is also helpful if you can give special instructions, ie, 'open brackets . . . close brackets', in a slightly different tone from your normal voice, so that they can be recognised as instructions and not typed by mistake.
3 Spell out foreign and unusual words, using the phonetic alphabet (if necessary) and pronounce difficult words slowly and clearly.
4 Keep the volume of your voice as low as practicable.
5 Hold the microphone fairly close to your mouth and speak directly into it.
6 Do not speak too quickly or in jerks. Speak at the speed used for dictating to a shorthand-typist.
7 Avoid clipping words using the 'on-off' switch.

At the conclusion of each passage:
1 Dictate the complimentary close.
2 If there are enclosures, state the size of envelope required.
3 If a correction has to be made, refer to it on the index slip.
4 Mark the index or slip to show the end of the passage.

At the conclusion of the whole dictation:
1 State that you are signing off.

When transcribing recorded dictation:

1 Pay attention to any special instructions and corrections accompanying the record.

2 Letters required urgently by the dictator should be typed, checked and returned to him first of all.

3 The size of each letter must be assessed before typing so that the correct size of paper is used.

4 Any doubtful points in the dictation should always be checked with the dictator or another responsible member of staff.

5 Consult a dictionary whenever there is any doubt about the spelling of a word.

6 Insert the proper punctuation marks and allow adequate paragraphs.

7 Every transcription must be accurately typed and the utmost care must be taken in checking letters, etc, before they are removed from the typewriter.

8 Take very great care of the transcribing machine and always cover it when not in use.

The illustration below is a centralised direct-link dictation system using the latest technique of computer logic. When someone picks up a telephone to dictate, the system electronically compares each typist's workload with her known typing speed. It then directs the caller to record directly on the unit of the typist able to do the work soonest. Typing turnround time is kept to a minimum with no break in work flow between author and typist.

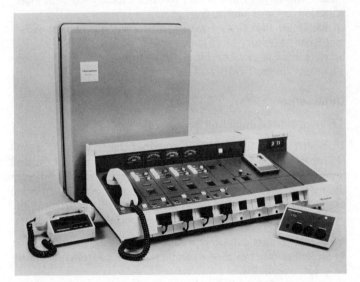

A centralised dictation system

On the system's control panel, dials show daily work input, output and current backlog for each typist's recorder unit and the turnround time which that backlog represents. This information is backed up by a continuous graph showing overall workloads. If a priority item is dictated, the typist can scan quickly forward to it and transcribe it out of sequence, while it is still being dictated if necessary. When the priority item has been typed, a digital counter guides the typist exactly to the point at which she interrupted her normal work. To clear a unit's work in an emergency, perhaps if a typist is ill, two typists can plug into one unit and simultaneously transcribe different items of work from the same tape.

Recording medium

Tapes are normally supplied in cassettes in the following sizes:
Universal (standard) cassette – 90 min each side
Micro-cassette – 60 min each side
Mini-cassette (for use on portable machines) – 20 min each side

Suppliers of dictation machines and accessories

Dictaphone Ltd, Alperton House, Bridgewater Road, Wembley, Middx HA0 1EH
Grundig International Ltd, 40–42 Newlands Park, Sydenham, London, SE26 5NQ
IBM United Kingdom, Ltd, 40 Basinghall Street, London EC2P 2DY
Lanier Business Products Inc, Rennell House, 40a Mill Place, Kingston-upon-Thames, Surrey
Office International (Group) Ltd, International House, Windmill Road, Sunbury-on-Thames, Middx TW16 7HR
Sony (UK) Ltd, Pyrene House, Sunbury Cross, Sunbury-on-Thames, Middx TW16 7AT

Duplicators

There are three duplicator processes:

1 **Spirit** A master copy (half-art paper coated with china clay) is prepared from a transfer sheet coated with an aniline dye and providing a mirror impression. The image is transferred from the master to the copy paper (now in positive form), spirit being used to dampen the copy paper and allow a small coating of the dye to be deposited on to the copies. Special features include:

• several colours can be reproduced at the same time
• limited number of copies can be reproduced from one master – 250 maximum
• masters can be hand-written, typed or prepared on a heat transfer copier

- this process is rarely used in business but educational establishments continue to use it for reproducing class materials

Correction of errors on masters: see p 32

2 Stencil A process in which ink is passed through indentations cut into a stencil. Special features include:

- copy paper is cheaper than the paper used in the other processes
- capable of reproducing up to 5000 copies
- photographs and drawings can be reproduced with electronic stencils
- separate runs and separate stencils are required for two or more colours
- suitable means of preparing circular letters, instruction manuals, house magazines, reports, agenda, minutes etc

Correction of errors on stencils: see p 32

Materials and ancillary equipment for stencil duplicating:

Stencils	– standard: for normal typing
	pre-cut: used for forms or letter headings
	tracing: translucent
	drawing: blue-coated for handwriting
	electronic: for reproducing diagrams and photographs
Pliafilm	– special plastic transparent sheet used to cover the stencil whilst it is being typed to keep the type bars free from wax
Ink	– supplied in tubes
Paper	– semi-absorbent
Correcting fluid	– for making corrections
Stylus pens and backing plates	– for handwriting
Blotting folders	– for storing stencils
Cardboard tops	– for fixing to stencils to store in vertical filing cabinets
Electronic stencil scanner	– machine which produces a facsimile stencil of an original drawing or photograph for duplicating. The stencil is cut by a sparking stylus which produces a facsimile. As an electronic eye (photocell) travels along the rotating copy, it emits signals from which a fine wire stylus cuts holes of varying size in the stencil according to the density of the copy

3 **Offset litho** The litho image on the plate is offset in negative form on to a rubber blanket and then transferred from the blanket into positive form on copy paper. The litho images on the plate accept ink but repel the water. Special features include:
- capable of reproducing large quantities, up to 50 000 copies from metal plates and 2000 copies from paper/plastic plates
- very good quality reproduction and copy paper
- suitable for preparing office forms, letter headings, leaflets, price lists, parts lists etc

Correction of errors on masters: see p 33

Materials for offset litho duplicating:

Fount solution	– solution of water and an additive
Ink	– ink, together with the fount solution, has to be applied very carefully in the right proportions; a polychrome ink gun may be used to dispense the ink
Etch	– liquid chemical applied to the plates to provide a film which attracts the ink to the image areas

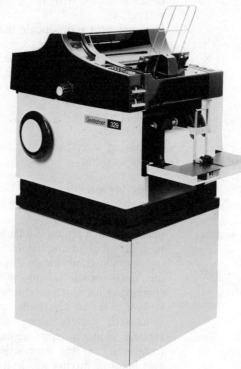

An offset litho duplicator

Blanket wash	– liquid which removes the impression from the blanket after each plate has been used
Blanket reviver	– highly inflammable liquid used to restore the surface of the blanket after a period of use
Paper	– any weight of paper may be used, but at least 85g is necessary if duplicating is required on both sides
Masters	– paper plates are normally prepared on an electrostatic plate maker but they can be typed with a litho ribbon; metal plates are prepared photographically by firms providing a plate-making service
Preserver	– liquid gum for protecting plates during storage

Suppliers of duplicators and accessories

AM International Information Systems Ltd, PO Box 17, Maylands Avenue, Hemel Hempstead, Herts HP2 7ET

A B Dick Ltd, PO Box 24, 88–95 High Street, Brentford, Middx TW8 8BA

Gestetner Ltd, PO Box 23, Gestetner House, 210 Euston Road, London NW1 2DA

Ozalid (UK) Ltd, Topasol House, Langston Road, Loughton, Essex IG10 3TH

Roneo Alcatel Ltd, PO Box 3, South Street, Romford, Essex RM1 2AR

Rotaprint Ltd, Rotaprint House, Honeypot Lane, London NW9 9RE

Typewriters and word processors

Equipment for producing words and text range from small manual, portable typewriters to word processors forming a part of an electronic mail system, as described below:

Portable typewriters Both manual and electric. They are compact and light – ideal for home use.

Standard typewriters Again both manual and electric, although manual typewriters are cheaper than the electric models. Electric models can be fitted with type bars or a cylindrical head 'golf ball', and have the following advantages over manual ones:

- less physical effort needed to operate them
- capable of making more carbon copies
- the electronically-controlled impression provides sharp, even striking of the keys ideal for cutting stencils and preparing masters

Self–correcting typewriters Typewriters fitted with an additional correcting ribbon which either covers the incorrect characters with a white deposit or removes them from the paper.

Taking care of your typewriter

1 Brush the type with a hard brush every morning.
2 Dust and clean the machine regularly.
3 Clean underneath the typewriter to stop dust rising into the machine.
4 When removing the cover, make sure that it is not caught up in some part of the mechanism.
5 Always cover the machine at night or whenever it is not in use.
6 If the typewriter has to be moved, lift it by the base from the back, and never by any other part. Before lifting, lock the carriage in the centre, preventing the carriage from running from one side to the other if the machine is tilted.
7 Never leave a typewriter:
   • near a hot radiator
   • where it can be knocked off the desk by a passer-by
8 Always use a backing sheet to protect the platen when using a single sheet of paper. The backing sheet will also improve the appearance of the typewriting.
9 When erasing, move the carriage fully to the left or right, using the margin-release key.
10 If the typewriter is not working properly, examine it and try to discover what is wrong. If the faulty part cannot be repaired easily or if the cause is not obvious, the machine should not be used until an experienced mechanic has attended to it.

Key questions to be answered when choosing a new typewriter:
1 What sort of work will be typed? Does it entail typing and calculating figures?
2 How many copies do you normally make?
3 What size are the documents?
4 Why does your present typewriter fail to satisfy your needs?
5 What type pitch and style are most effective for your requirements and do you need to vary these at all?
6 What correction facilities do you require?
7 Do you prepare masters/stencils for duplicating, copying or addressing machine work?
8 Do you type much repetitive work and use standard paragraphs?
9 Do you require any special characters or symbols?
10 What type of ribbon/ribbon carrier do you use in your organisation?

Electronic typewriters and magnetic card composers
These machines record characters in a memory as the operator
types. The typist can amend the contents of the memory by
adding or deleting material where required. Errors are corrected
by back-spacing and overtyping. When a piece of work has
been typed in its final form it can either be automatically
printed on paper and cleared from the memory, or transferred
to a magnetic card disc or tape for permanent storage. Features
include:
- justified margins
- daisy wheel printing elements which can easily be changed for
  different type styles and sizes
- automatic centring

Word processors

Word processors are screen-based systems, ie the operator's key
actions are displayed on a screen. The amount displayed varies
between full-page, half-page and single-line according to the
type of word processor. Word processors are either operated as a
stand-alone system or a shared logic system. The stand-alone
system has its own microcomputer and is a self-contained unit
with a visual display unit and keyboard, memory and printer. In
the shared logic system there are several work stations with visual
display units and keyboards, each sharing a single central
processor and one or more printers.

Word processors are normally capable of:
1 Editing text on the screen by inserting new material and
   deleting unwanted material.
2 Displaying 'prompts' to guide the operator.
3 Adding or deleting paragraphs.
4 Moving words, sentences, paragraphs and columns to other
   parts of the page.
5 Automatic numbering of pages.
6 Justifying margins.
7 Automatic decimal alignment.
8 Scrolling text vertically and horizontally on the screen.
9 Holding data in a buffer store for later use.
10 Allowing documents to be merged or a mailing list to be
   merged with a circular letter.
11 Printing one page of a document whilst the operator is
   typing the next page.
Refinements include:
1 Revealing the bottom line of a preceding page and the top
   line of the following page on the screen at the same time.
2 Checking the spelling of words against a built-in 'dictionary'.
3 Using word processors in electronic mail systems for transmitting documents direct from one word processor to
   another in different parts of the world.

Common applications for word processors:
1   Automatic typing of standard letters merged with a mailing
    list to provide selected names and addresses.
2   Updating price lists, telephone directories, mailing lists,
    parts lists where amendments can be made and inserted
    without retyping all of the matter.
3   Typing the drafts of reports, minutes, articles etc. Once the
    draft has been typed, the typist can make amendments as
    required and the machine automatically reformats the pages
    without any further retyping and checking.

A word processor

Suppliers of typewriters and word processors

AM Jacquard Systems Ltd, Times House, Station Approach,
Ruislip, Middx HA4 8LE
British Olivetti Ltd, 30 Berkeley Square, London W1X 6AG
Data Recall Ltd, Sondes Place, Dorking, Surrey RH4 3EF
Facit-Addo Ltd, Maidstone Road, Rochester, Kent ME1 3QN
Hermes Precisal Ltd, Centurion House, St Johns Street,
Colchester, Essex CO2 7AH
IBM United Kingdom Ltd, 40 Basinghall Street, London
EC2P 2DY
Imperial Business Equipment Ltd, Imperial House, 133–149
St Nicholas Circle, Leicester LE1 4LE
Nexos (United Kingdom) Ltd, UDS House, 3 Jefferson Way,
Thame, Oxon OX9 3SU
Olympia Business Machines Ltd, 203–205 Old Marylebone
Road, London NW1 5QS

Philips Electronic & Associated Industries Ltd, Arundel Great Court, 8 Arundel Street, London WC2R 3DT
Wang (UK) Ltd, 211–217 Lower Richmond Road, Richmond, Surrey TW9 4LU
Wordplex Ltd, Europe Assistance House, 252 High Street, Croydon CR0 1NF

Office furniture and layout

Office furniture should be carefully chosen as it contributes to the health, welfare and safety of employees as well as increasing efficiency and making the most effective use of space. Furniture for the modern electronic office should be of the purpose-built type, to cater for the needs of people operating such equipment as VDUs, word processors, computers, microfilm equipment, etc. Several finishes are available but the choice is usually between wood, plastic or metal.

Provision also has to be made for cabling which should be as unobtrusive as possible. Wiring channels can be incorporated in desks so that telephones and lighting can be positioned in convenient places without having trailing cables.

The secretary's office will usually be located in one of the following positions:
• a separate 'cellular' office adjoining the boss's office
• a work area in the boss's own office
• a work area in an open plan office
Whichever of these positions you occupy, the working environment, furniture requirements and layout are much the same and in planning your office bear in mind the following:

Work flow Occupy a position as near as possible to your boss's office to reduce the amount of walking between the two offices.

Space Allow enough space for working. The Health and Safety at Work Act specifies a minimum 3.715 square metres per person.

Desk situation For security reasons, position your desk so that visitors will not be able to read confidential documents in your typewriter. If you are in an office with others it is not a good idea to be face-to-face with another person.

Lighting Correct lighting is important in creating the right conditions. Position it carefully to spread the light evenly across work surfaces. Also remember that a VDU emits light as well as reflecting it, so it should be positioned so that reflections do not shine into your eyes.

Systems furniture for the secretary

Systems furniture with a VDU table and keyboard well

Layout This should be balanced and pleasing, boosting morale and prestige.

Noise If possible, isolate noisy machines in a separate office or screen them off with soundproof panels.

Equipment Filing cabinets, telephones etc should be positioned within easy reach. However, do not place cabinets so that extended drawers obstruct a passageway.

Display Use pinboards, visual control boards, display areas etc for displaying information which you use frequently. These provide good memory aids and are easily accessible.

Decor Create a pleasing environment which reflects your own personality by displaying a favourite picture, photograph, pot plant etc, but if you have some form of greenery remember to water it!

Furniture The size and design of desks should take account of office technological equipment, including telephones, VDU keyboard, microfilm equipment and dictation machine. Specially-adapted work surfaces are required with provision for cable channels and plugs. Measurements for office desks and chairs are recommended in the British Standards Institution specification BS 5940: 1980.

Suppliers of office furniture

Abbotts Bros (Southall) Ltd, Abbess House, High Street, Southall, Middx UB1 3HE

Carson Office Furniture Ltd, 36 Croydon Road, Beckenham, Kent BR3 4BH

Du-al Furniture Ltd, Williamstown, Tonypandy, Mid Glamorgan, South Wales CF40 1NF

Leabank Office Equipment PLC, Vastre Industrial Estate, Kerry Road, Newton, Powys SY16 1DZ

Martela Contract Interiors Ltd, 210 High Holborn, London WC1V 7BP

Herman Miller Ltd, Lower Bristol Road, Bath BA2 2ER

Project Office Furniture Ltd, Hamlet Green, Haverhill, Suffolk CB9 8QJ

Ryman Ltd, 6–10 Great Portland Street, London W1N 6DL

Sheer Pride Ltd, Weybridge Trading Estate, Addlestone Road, Weybridge, Surrey

Tan-Sad Ltd, Lodge Causeway, Fishponds, Bristol BS16 3JU

Petty cash

Key factors in recording petty cash:

1 The imprest (or float), £50 in the example on p 114, should always be the value of the petty cash vouchers plus cash in hand.

2 At the beginning of the period, the imprest is the balance of cash brought forward from the previous period plus any cash received.

PETTY CASH BOOK

Dr.   Cr.

Received	Date	Folio	Details	V'r no	Total paid out	Stationery	Cleaning	Postage	Office sundries	VAT
	198-									
5 60	Jan 1		Balance b/f							
44 40	" 1	CB1	Cash received							
	" 2		Adhesive tape	119	1 61	1 40				21
	" 8		Newspapers	120	8 65				8 65	
	" 9		Cleaning materials	121	2 78		2 42			36
	" 10		Air letter forms	122	1 60			1 60		
	" 15		Registered envelopes	123	7 80			7 80		
	" 22		Pot plant	124	5 00				5 00	
	" 23		Laundry	125	6 25		6 25			
	" 25		Typewriter ribbons	126	14 49	12 60				1 89
					48 18	14 00	8 67	9 40	13 65	2 46
	" 31		Balance c/f		1 82	L7	L2	L3	L4	L5
50 00					50 00					
1 82	Feb 1		Balance b/f							
48 18	" 1	CB2	Cash received							

Page from a petty cash book

3   To calculate the amount needed to restore the imprest at the end of the period, subtract the balance of cash in hand from the imprest. This amount should equal the total payments.
4   Every item of expenditure should be entered twice in the petty cash account; once in the total column and once in the appropriate analysis column.
5   When totalling the columns at the end of a period, the total of all analysis columns should be equal to the total payments column.
6   Whenever cash is paid out, a receipt or voucher should be obtained.
7   Petty cash vouchers are signed twice; once by the person who spends the money and once by a person who is authorised to approve the expenditure.
8   The vouchers should be numbered as they are received and filed numerically for audit purposes; the voucher numbers being entered in the petty cash account to facilitate reference to the documents.
9   The analysis columns are not always the same and can be varied to suit individual requirements.
10 The cash box should be locked when not in use.

Postal mail services

Air letter forms Specially designed forms for sending letters abroad by airmail at a cheap postage rate, but not suitable for enclosures.

Airmail letters/cards/parcels Sending letters, cards and parcels abroad by airmail to most destinations. Must contain a blue airmail label.

Airway letters Transmitting letters by British Airways on certain domestic flights.

All-up Letters and cards for Europe go by air or surface mail, whichever is the quicker.

Business reply Enables a person to receive 1st and 2nd class cards or letters from correspondents without putting them to the expense of paying postage.

Cash on delivery Collecting cash from the addressee on delivery of a parcel.

Compensation fee parcel A parcel service which provides compensation if lost or damaged.

Data post An overnight package delivery service from door to door. Also suitable for sending urgent packages overseas.

Direct bag Transmitting a bag of mail or goods to an individual address in the United Kingdom or abroad.

Express post A fast messenger collection and delivery service available in London and certain other large towns and cities.

First-class letters/cards For urgent mail. It will normally be delivered on the first working day after collection.

Freepost Enables a person to receive replies by 2nd class post from correspondents without putting them to the expense of paying postage. They are required to quote a special freepost address.

Intelpost Special electronic transmission of documents by fac-simile telegraphy.

Late posted packets Posting boxes provided on mail trains for the acceptance of late mail.

Newspapers Special service which enables publications reg-istered as newspapers to be given first-class service at cheaper rates of postage.

Overseas printed papers Sending printed papers abroad by airmail or surface mail at reduced rates of postage.

Overseas small packets Transmitting goods, including trade samples, whether dutiable or not, in the same mail as printed papers, which normally travel quicker than parcel mails.

Parcels Transmitting articles up to a maximum weight of 10 kg.

Postage forward parcels Enables a person to receive parcels from correspondents without putting them to the expense of paying postage.

Poste restante Letters and parcels addressed to a post office to be collected by a person without a fixed address.

Private bags Lockable private bags which may be used for the posting and receipt of mail.

Private boxes Private boxes which may be rented at a normal delivery post office for the reception of postal packets to be collected by the users as an alternative to delivery by postmen.

Railway letters Conveying first-class letters by train – handed in at a railway station.

Railway parcels Conveying parcels by train – handed in at an express delivery post office.

Recorded delivery Service for the correspondent who requires not only proof of posting but, if necessary, proof of delivery.

Registered letters Sending articles of value and providing for compensation if lost.

Reply coupons Used internationally for prepaying replies from correspondents. Reply coupons are exchangeable for postage stamps at post offices abroad.

Second-class letters/cards Cheaper service for letters/cards which will normally be delivered up to the third working day after collection.

Second-class letters posted in bulk Rebate of postage is allowed on second-class letters posted in bulk when the number exceeds 4250.

Selectapost The post office arranges to sort mail into specified categories before it is delivered.

Special delivery Special priority next-day delivery of letters.

Swiftair Special high-speed overseas letter post which delivers airmail letters at least one day earlier than those sent by ordinary airmail or the all-up service.

Reference sources:
Post Office Guide and *Supplements*
Postal Rates Inland Compendium
Postal Rates Overseas Compendium

Printing

Preparation and correction of printed matter

Key factors when typing matter to be printed:

1 Type on one side of the paper only, with double spacing and with a two-inch margin at the left-hand side of each sheet.
2 Number the pages consecutively.
3 Type footnotes immediately following the line containing the reference. Use headings within chapters to break up the text into convenient sections. Where more than one type of heading is used, their relative importance should be clearly indicated, eg section heading, subheading, sub-subheading etc, so that these variations may be interpreted typographically with the correct emphasis.
4 When sending 'copy' for printing state your requirements, such as type sizes, quality of paper, colour, size and the quantity required, etc.
5 The printer supplies a 'pull' or set of proofs before he carries out the actual printing. No major alterations should be carried out on the proof. This will involve the printer in a considerable amount of work and of course the cost will be increased.

No	Correction	Sign in margin	Sign in text
1	Insert full stop	⊙	⋏
2	Insert colon	⊙	⋏
3	Insert comma	,/	⋏
4	Insert semi-colon	;/	⋏
5	Insert question mark	?/	⋏
6	Insert exclamation mark	!/	⋏
7	Insert apostrophe	ʾ	⋏
8	Insert quotation marks	ʾ ʾ	⋏ ⋏
9	Insert hyphen	⊢⊣	⋏
10	Insert dash	/–/	⋏
11	Insert brackets	(/)/	⋏ ⋏
12	Insert square brackets	[/]/	⋏ ⋏
13	Use capital letters	Caps	≡
14	Use small capital letters	SC	
15	Underline word(s)	Underline	
16	Insert word(s)	Words to be inserted /	⋏
17	Use italics	ital	
18	Use Roman type	Rom	encircle word(s)
19	Use bold type	Bold	∼∼∼
20	Use lower case letters	l c	encircle letter(s)
21	Transpose words or letters	trs	Word(s) or letter(s)
22	Delete	⌿	crossed out
23	To remain as it was before correction	Stet	········ under word(s) to remain
24	Space required	#	⋏
25	Equalise the spacing	•q #	⋏
26	Close up the space	⌒	⌒
27	Start a new paragraph	N P	⌈
28	Continue without a new paragraph	Run on	
29	Improve damaged character	×	encircle character
30	Wrong fount	w.f.	encircle character
31	Letter upside down	ꝺ	encircle character
32	Move to the left	⌐	⌐
33	Move to the right	⌐	⌐
34	Place in the centre	Centre	⌐⌐ indicating position
35	Raise line	Raise	
36	Lower line	Lower	
37	Straighten margin	‖	‖
38	Passage omitted	Out see copy	
39	Remove printer's space	⊥	encircle space
40	Abbreviation or figure to be printed in full	Spell out	encircle words or figures

Printer's correction signs

Key factors when checking proofs:

1 Check the proof very carefully with the 'copy'.
2 Mark the proof clearly with the correct signs – a table giving the usual printers' correction signs is given above.
3 Mark every error in the margin and in the text itself.
4 On a second copy, repeat all the correction marks made on the first. This copy should be retained for reference purposes.
5 If a second proof is required, mark the corrected proof 'Revise'. If the first proof is quite satisfactory and no further proofs are required, mark it 'Press' or 'Press after correction' (where minor corrections have been made).

Below is a printer's proof with a selection of the correction signs given in the previous table. The numbers refer to the signs given in the table. A full list of printers' correction signs is given in *Printers' Correction Signs* (BS 5261: 1975/1976).

Centre

Caps
Spell out

⌐   ⌐

Fulbridge Manufacturing Company Limited

The (10th Ord. Gen.) Meeting of Fulbridge Manufacturing
Company Limited was held recently in Bristol. [Mr. Hugh
Watkins, the Chairman, presided and, in the course of his
speech, said It is pleasing for the Directors to be able once
again to report record trading profits these, I may say have
been achieved under the most difficult circumstances when
prices of raw materials have shown marked changes from
time to time, and when the prices of some metals which we
have to buy in very large quantities have increased consider-
ably. This striving after the highest possible production
has been the company's regular policy since 1950. At the
present time we are proud to say we have not passed on
any increases to our customers since the last general increase
took place nearly four years ago.

I am sorry to say that the prices of all our new commodities
are still rising, the demands of all branches of labour for
higher wages are increasing, and if these movements continue we shall, of course, sooner or later be compelled to
pass on some part of these increased costs.

The financial position of the company is, I think you will
agree, very strong. Adequate stocks of materials are available and we are making steady progress towards improving
the position of our deliveries.

Perhaps our greatest difficulty has been to obtain sufficient
labour for our requirements, and to meet this position we
have spent large sums on the provision of mechanized new
equipment and also on the improved production methods
in each of our factories, and we are now benefiting from
these changes.

You will also be pleased to know that your New Zealand
Branch has shown remarkable progress during this year.

A printer's proof with corrections marked

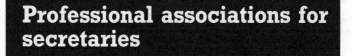

Professional associations for secretaries

Association of Legal Secretaries
Address: 46 Orchard Way, Woodhatch, Reigate, Surrey
Publication: *Legal Secretary*

Association of Medical Secretaries
Address: Tavistock House South, Tavistock Square, London
               WC1H 9LN
Publication: *The Medical Secretary and Receptionist*

Association of Personal Assistants and Secretaries Ltd
Address: 14 Victoria Terrace, Leamington Spa, Warwickshire
Publication: APAS News

European Association of Professional Secretaries
Address: 8 rue de la Michodière, 75083 Paris   Cedex 02
Publication: EAPS Brief

Executive Secretaries Association
Address: 45 Milford Close, Abbey Wood, London SE2 0DS
Publication: National Quarterly Newsletter

Institute of Agricultural Secretaries
Address: 1 Main Street, Elloughton, Brough, North Humberside HU15 1JN
Publication: Newsletter and Bulletin

Institute of Qualified Private Secretaries
Address: 126 Farnham Road, Slough, Bucks SL1 4XA
Publication: The IQPS Journal

Public relations

Although only large organisations will normally employ a public relations officer or use the services of a public relations agency, no organisation can ignore the need to establish good relationships with the public, as well as with those associated with the organisation.

A secretary can influence public relations in the following ways:

- receiving visitors in a friendly and efficient manner (see p 123)
- being courteous and helpful with telephone callers (see p 135)
- paying attention to neatness, style and tone in the preparation of correspondence and replying promptly to letters received
- pride in personal appearance
- keeping a tidy and well-organised office
- maintaining good communications both within and outside the organisation through house magazines, press reports, broadcasts etc
- being punctual for appointments and meetings, and efficient in making arrangements for them
- establishing good relationships with employees and organising social events for them

- cultivating and maintaining friendly contacts with local organisations involving traders and the community in general

Further information concerning a career in, and the role of, public relations is obtainable from The Institute of Public Relations.

Qualifications for secretaries

The chief examining bodies offering private secretarial examinations, ie the Business Education Council, the London Chamber of Commerce and Industry, Pitman Examinations Institute and the Royal Society of Arts, all recognise the need for private secretaries not only to be highly skilled in shorthand-typewriting, but to have a sound knowledge and understanding of business and secretarial subjects. A brief description follows of each of the examinations suitable for secretaries. Students who wish to progress to senior positions should seek to qualify at the highest level.

Business Education Council

This Council, which administers business education in England and Wales (and SCOTBEC for Scotland), has recognised the need for a national system of awards which reflect levels of secretarial skills within the context of a broad business education. Those gaining BEC awards should be able to fill positions involving a greater degree of initiative and responsibility than mere typing and shorthand skills.

At national level, ie for those with at least four GCE 'O' level qualifications or equivalent, the two-year course for secretarial students contains the following modules:

Year 1	*Year 2*
People and communication	Quantitative and accounting
Numeracy and accounting	methods
Organisation in its environment	Administration in business
ment	Organisation in its environment
Secretarial skills	ment
(double module)	Secretarial skills
Optional business study	(double module)
	Secretarial services

The secretarial services module should enable the student to work effectively as a secretary and give her the knowledge, skills and understanding for her career.

By taking the BEC national level course, secretarial students should acquire the necessary educational base for a range of careers in business. It provides the student not only with the necessary secretarial skills but, if desired, a chance to branch out into other business careers. Similar courses are offered at the higher national levels for students with the national qualification or GCE 'A' levels.

For further details write to: The Business Education Council, Berkshire House, 168–173 High Holborn, London WC1V 7AG.

The London Chamber of Commerce and Industry

Three levels of grouped secretarial examinations are offered.

Secretarial Studies Certificate – intended for those who seek employment as junior secretaries and shorthand-typists. The examinations consist of: Communications; Background to business; Office practice; Shorthand-typewriting or Audio-typewriting (a recording).

Private Secretary's Certificate – intended for those who seek employment as private secretaries to middle-management. The examinations consist of: Communications; Office organisation and secretarial procedures; Structure of business; Shorthand-typewriting duties or Audio-typewriting duties (a recording).

Private Secretary's Diploma – set at a higher level than the certificate examination and is intended for senior secretaries wishing to be employed by top-level management. The examination consists of six sections: Communications; Private secretarial duties; Management appreciation; Meetings (a video recording); Shorthand-typewriting duties (a recording); and an Interview.

For further details write to: The London Chamber of Commerce and Industry, Commercial Education Scheme, Marlowe House, Station Road, Sidcup, Kent DA15 6BJ.

Pitman Examinations Institute

A range of examinations appropriate for shorthand-typists and secretaries is offered, including the following:

Private Secretarial Duties (Intermediate) – tests the candidate's knowledge of the main duties of a private secretary, both as part of an organisation and also in relation to the broader business world. The private secretary must carry out secretarial tasks efficiently, and supervise or direct junior staff. Candidates need to be aware of all social and business matters they might meet and display an ability to work on their own initiative.

Higher Secretarial Group Certificate – an award recognising all-round secretarial efficiency. Five subjects are examined, including private secretarial duties. For further details write to: Pitman Examinations Institute, Godalming, Surrey GU7 1UU.

Royal Society of Arts

The Society offers single-subject examinations as well as a group certificate, as follows:

The **Diploma for Personal Assistants** – a senior secretarial qualification for personal assistants. It provides a suitable background of knowledge and skills, and encourages the development of self-confidence and initiative, so that the student will come to play a responsible role in an administrative environment.

The examinations are arranged under two main headings:

Administration	*Communication*
Economic and financial aspects	Written
Legal aspects	Office skills applied (a recording)
Personnel and functional aspects	Oral

Secretarial Duties Stage II – a single-subject examination, assessing knowledge of secretarial duties and the ability to apply this knowledge at the level of a potential secretary.

For further details write to: Royal Society of Arts (Publications), Murray Road, Orpington, Kent BR5 3RB.

Reception

The visitor gains his first impression of the organisation when he is received by the receptionist or secretary, and this is very important. A favourable impression is created when:
1 The reception office is tastefully furnished and tidy. Decorative plants enhance the appearance of an office.
2 The receptionist or secretary is pleasant, polite, helpful, smart and well-spoken.
3 The visitor is made welcome and well looked after, eg:
   ● invite him to sit in an easy chair while waiting
   ● supply him with an appropriate newspaper/journal to read
   ● if there is a delay, apologise and offer a cup of coffee or tea and keep him fully informed of the position

4 A record is kept of callers expected and callers received (a register of callers or visitors book will normally be compiled – see below).

5 The visitor is introduced correctly to the firm's representative by announcing his name, title and company clearly. Give the visitor's name before the name of your firm's representative, but when introducing a man and a woman, it is courteous to announce the woman's name first.

6 The receptionist uses the visitor's name during conversation with him. The efficient receptionist or secretary will know by name the visitors who call regularly.

7 The receptionist is tactful and helpful when a visitor (without an appointment) cannot see the person requested. In these circumstances, arrangements are made for the visitor to see someone else or another appointment is arranged on a mutually agreed date.

8 The receptionist has a thorough knowledge of the organisation, its activities and personnel, and can supply information to visitors without having to consult others.

9 Full information is immediately available concerning the organisation, as well as local hotels, train/air services, telephone numbers etc.

Date	Name of caller	Organisation	Time of arrival	Referred to
19 – –				
Feb 1	P R Francis	Barker Bros	0930	J Smith
" 1	K Clarke	Cannock College of FE	0945	R Payne
" 1	Dr T Berner	Werner e Wudt	1015	G R Docherty

Register of callers

Reports

Always aim to present facts accurately, clearly, concisely and in a logical order. If the report is a personal one between two persons, ie from the secretary to the personnel manager, it should be written in the first person. If it is of a meeting, it should be written wholly in the third person. A report of an event or a meeting should always be written in the past tense.

Before writing a report, prepare a plan and group the facts or ideas in a logical sequence, as follows:

1   The heading or title containing:
    - the subject of the report, eg the type of meeting
    - the date of the meeting or event
    - the place
    - if a meeting, those present – identifying the chairman and officers
    - a file reference number for future identification
    - the name of the person to whom the report is sent
    - any security classification, eg confidential or secret
2   The opening paragraph, which should state the terms of reference or the circumstances which called for the report, eg the personnel manager's memo, or changing circumstances which called for the discussion of future policy.
3   The body of the report containing the facts of the case or the major points discussed at a meeting. Use subheadings to divide the main topics.
4   Recommendations or conclusions.
5   State the action necessary to carry out the recommendations, including:
    - the names of the persons who should take the action
    - the date by which the action should be taken
    - the date of the next meeting to review the situation
6   The name and description of the signatory (unless this is incorporated in the heading).

Safety and accident prevention in the office

Safety and accident prevention is the concern and responsibility of us all. See the duties of employees required by the Health and Safety at Work Act 1974 on p 79.

Office layout and organisation

1 Plan your office layout to reduce the danger of accidents caused by poorly sited furniture and equipment or obstructions in gangways or corridors.

2 Avoid opening a heavy top drawer of a vertical filing cabinet because the whole cabinet is liable to topple over. It is advisable to open the bottom drawer before the top drawer to serve as a prop and lessen the risk. Load all the drawers evenly and, if possible, avoid placing heavy files in the top one.

3 Do not stand on a swivel chair to reach a file or other object placed in a high position: use a secure step-ladder.

4 Avoid putting portable heaters where they might cause an obstruction or a fire.

Use of equipment

1 Handle equipment as instructed and switch off machines and remove plugs when not in use.

2 Avoid having a trailing flex from a socket to a machine which can be a hazard for the operator and passers-by.

3 Regular care and maintenance of equipment is necessary. If a machine does not work properly, do not tamper with electrical parts but call a mechanic.

4 Report to your supervisor without delay any faults in equipment or frayed flexes.

5 Be aware of the dangers of dangling jewellery and long hair when operating certain machines and take the necessary remedial action.

6 Check that dangerous parts of machinery are fitted with guards, especially paper-cutting machines, and that the correct operating procedures are used.

7 Make sure that equipment is placed securely on desks and tables.

Fire precautions

1 Make sure that you and your colleagues know what to do should a fire break out, eg how to raise the fire alarm; how to use fire-fighting equipment if required to do so; and which escape route and assembly point to use.
2 Keep fire doors closed when not in use.
3 Do not smoke in any part of the building where there is a risk of fire. When in the office, make sure that smokers use ash-trays and not the waste-paper bin or floor.
4 Many of the correcting and cleaning fluids give off a highly inflammable vapour. After use, immediately replace the stopper. Make sure that inflammable materials, such as cans of spirit, are locked away in a well-ventilated store room when not in use.
5 Insist upon combustible materials such as papers and envelopes being placed in waste bins and that they are removed regularly for disposal.

First-aid

Make sure that you know who the first-aider is in your organisation and the position of the first-aid cabinet or sick room (see also pp 49–51).

BE CONSCIOUS OF SAFETY AT ALL TIMES!

Publications on safety

Is my Office Safe? A handbook for supervisors, HMSO.
Health and Safety at Work etc Act 1974. Advice to Employees, Health and Safety Commission.
Various publications from The British Safety Council, National Safety Centre, Chancellor's Road, London W6 9RS, and The Fire Protection Association, Aldermary House, Queen Street, London EC4N 1TJ.

Security

Key factors for safeguarding confidential information, cash, property and people's lives.

Confidentiality of information

1 Make sure that records containing confidential information are housed in locked filing cabinets or cupboards when not in use.

2 Confidential information recorded on tapes and discs for use on dictating machines, word processors and computers should receive the same security treatment as documents.

3 Take special care of carbon paper and carbon ribbons used when typing confidential documents as it is possible to detect information from them.

4 Mark confidential documents and envelopes clearly to indicate their security category.

5 Burn or destroy with a shredder any secret or confidential documents no longer required.

6 If you are asked for confidential information by an unauthorised person, tactfully evade the question and suggest that enquiries should be made elsewhere.

7 If you have to reproduce confidential documents on a duplicator or copier, supervise the work yourself so that the contents are not seen by others.

Cash handling

1 Keep cash and other valuables locked in a safe.
2 Arrange for money to be paid into a bank as soon as possible after receipt to avoid holding large sums of money in the office.
3 Large sums of money should be transported to and from the bank by a security agency. However, if this is undertaken by your staff, two people should go using specially designed cash-carrying cases equipped with smoke/dye alarms.
4 Spot checks should be made regularly on any transactions involving the transfer of money.

Access to buildings

Common methods used to control access to buildings by staff and visitors:

1 Locking doors to offices with central control of keys.
2 Visitors' book.
3 Identity passes. Magnetic or infra-red coded cards are used by staff in some organisations to gain entry to buildings where security is essential.
4 Large firms employ security officers to control admission of visitors and maintenance staff.
5 Closed-circuit television for observation of buildings.
6 A broadcasting system used for staff announcements and personnel location during the day can be reversed at night to perform a sound-detection system.

Bomb scares

Postal packages If you receive a suspicious package in the post, eg unusual shape or size, with wires attached to it, or with grease marks on the cover,

Do not:
- attempt to open it or allow anyone else to handle it
- put it in sand or water or in a container
- press or prod it in any way

But do:
- handle the package gently, placing it on a flat surface above floor level and away from a corner of the office
- leave the office as soon as possible, lock the door and hold on to the key for use by the police when they arrive
- inform your security or safety officer and the police (dial 999) immediately
- keep the entrance to the office clear of people

Telephone calls If you receive a telephone call stating that a bomb has been planted on the premises, you should try to get as much information as possible from the caller, such as:
- location of the bomb
- time it is expected to go off
- any circumstances concerning the motive for the bomb
- identity of the caller

Make as many notes as possible of the conversation and try to detect the nationality and any accent of the informer. Immediately after the call:

a inform your security or safety officer and the police (dial 999)
b assist the security or safety officer to take the necessary precautions until the police arrive to take charge of the situation.

Manufacturers of security equipment and devices

C W Cave & Co Ltd, 5 Tenter Road, Moulton Park Industrial Estate, Northants NN3 1PZ

Chubb & Sons Lock and Safe Ltd, 14–22 Tottenham Street, London W1P 0AA

Envopak Group Sales Ltd, Powerscroft Road, Sidcup, Kent DA14 5EF

Securikey Ltd, PO Box 18, Aldershot, Hants GU12 6JX

Todd Research Ltd, Robjohns Road, Chelmsford, Essex CM1 3DP

Volumatic Ltd, Taurus House, Kingfield Road, Coventry CV6 5AS

Seeking and starting a new job

Sources

To find out information about job vacancies, consult:

Careers offices
Job centres
Staffing agencies
Newspapers
Firm's noticeboard or staff bulletin for internal vacancies

Applying for a vacancy

Great care should be taken in preparing the letter of application for a post so that the prospective employer will be favourably impressed. When writing your letter, bear in mind the following points:

1 Write the letter in your best handwriting, unless a typed letter has been specially requested.
2 The letter should be neat, free from grammatical or punctuation errors, and businesslike (see Correspondence, p 34).
3 The source of the advertisement should be referred to, eg if it appeared in the *Southern Evening Echo*, write 'In reply to your advertisement in yesterday's Southern Evening Echo . . .'
4 Plan the letter carefully, covering all the essential points asked for or further particulars.
5 The salutation should normally be 'Dear Sir' or 'Dear Madam' and the complimentary close 'Yours faithfully'.
6 It is usual to attach a curriculum vitae supplying the following details:
   • full name, address and telephone number
   • date of birth
   • education
   • examination successes (include grades with GCE and CSE results)
   • additional training and qualifications for the post
   • present employment and previous experience of office work
   • names and addresses of persons to whom reference may be made
7 If you receive a letter inviting you to attend for interview, reply by return of post confirming that you will be pleased to attend at the stated time.

The interview

When attending an interview:

Do

- Be prepared by finding out as much as possible about the organisation and the vacancy you are after, ie read the job description carefully, if one has been supplied.
- Pay particular attention to your appearance – clothes, hair etc are smart and tidy.
- Be punctual, demonstrating your ability to be well-organised.

- Bring with you any documents, writing materials, etc which were requested in the letter.
- Be perfectly natural and speak clearly and deliberately.
- Be pleasant – a smile always creates a favourable impression.
- Make the most of the subjects which you have experience or knowledge of.
- Be perfectly honest about your capabilities and achievements, drawing attention to any which support your application.

- Show that you are interested and enthusiastic by your attitude to the questions asked.

Don't

- Waste the interviewer's time by attending when you have no intention of accepting.

- Wear clothes which are not usually worn in an office.

- Rush the journey so that you arrive agitated and ill-prepared to answer questions calmly.
- Bring your raincoat, umbrella, etc into the interview room – leave them outside in the waiting room.
- Sit down in the interview room until you are invited to do so.
- Be afraid to look at the interviewer.

- Discuss irrelevancies, departing from the point of a question.
- Question the interviewer, but be prepared to ask questions if you are invited to do so. You may wish to have more information about job prospects, salary, terms of employment etc.
- Fiddle with your handkerchief, handbag, etc while you are being interviewed – it can distract and annoy the interviewer.

Accepting an offer of employment

If you receive a letter offering you a job, it is important to reply as soon as possible informing the employer of your acceptance or rejection. If you are accepting the offer, confirm that you will begin on the date suggested.

Starting the new job

Adequate and thorough preparation for a new post is essential if you are to get off to a good start, eg:

1 Be punctual – plan the necessary travel arrangements so that you are familiar with the route to your new employment.
2 Make sure that you have your income tax form P45 and any other documents requested, such as birth certificate or medical certificate.
3 When you start, enquire about the firm's style of display for correspondence and your boss's personal preferences.
4 Get to know as quickly as possible people's names and their positions in the firm; the location and function of offices/ departments and the special requirements of your job. Most firms organise an induction course for new staff and this will help you to acquire essential information about the firm and your place in it.
5 Note the duties placed upon you by the Health and Safety at Work Act (see p 79).
6 Within 13 weeks of beginning your job you should be given a written contract of employment (see p 81).

Stationery

Examples of some common uses for the different sizes of paper:
A3 – legal documents
    balance sheets and financial statements
A4 – business letters, reports, minutes, agenda, specifications, bills of quantities, estimates, quotations, invoices
A5 – short letters, memos, invoices (small), credit notes, statements
A6 – post cards, index cards, requisitions, petty cash vouchers, compliment slips
A7 – business visiting cards, labels

Paper quantities

Quire = 25 sheets (formerly 24)
Ream = 500 sheets (formerly 480)

International paper sizes

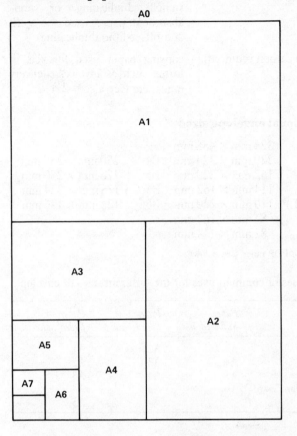

Sizes

A0 = 841 mm × 1189 mm
A1 = 594 mm × 841 mm
A2 = 420 mm × 594 mm
A3 = 297 mm × 420 mm

A4 = 210 mm × 297 mm
A5 = 148 mm × 210 mm
A6 = 105 mm × 148 mm
A7 = 74 mm × 105 mm

International paper sizes

Types of paper

Bond
— a good quality paper used for headed paper and 'top-copy' work

Bank (flimsy)
— a cheaper and lighter grade used for carbon copies and sets of forms

Airmail
— very thin (lightweight) paper for correspondence sent by airmail

Duplicating	– semi-absorbent paper used for stencil duplicating or non-absorbent paper used for spirit and offset-litho duplicating

NCR (no carbon required)
Carbon-free ⎤ – copying paper used for sets of
⎦ forms such as invoices, delivery notes, etc (see also p 21)

International envelope sizes

C3	324 mm × 458 mm		
C4	229 mm × 324 mm	B4	250 mm × 353 mm
C5	162 mm × 229 mm	B5	176 mm × 250 mm
C6*	114 mm × 162 mm	B6/C4	125 mm × 324 mm
C5/6 (DL)*	110 mm × 220 mm	B6	125 mm × 176 mm
C7/6	81 mm × 162 mm		
C7	81 mm × 114 mm		

* Within the POP range (see below)

Examples of common uses for the different sizes of envelope:

Envelope	Paper unfolded	Paper folded once	Paper folded twice
C3	A3	A2	A1
C4 or B4	A4	A3	A2
C5 or B5	A5	A4	A3
C6 or B6 or C5/6	A6	A5	A4
C7/6			A5

Post Office Preferred (POP) envelopes

The Post Office has the power to state that, in future, only the Post Office Preferred range of envelopes and cards will be accepted for the lowest postage rates. To fall within the preferred range, envelopes and cards should be at least 90 mm × 140 mm and not larger than 120 mm × 235 mm.

Types of envelopes

Banker – the opening is on the longer side

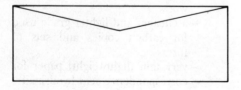

Pocket   – the opening is on the shorter side

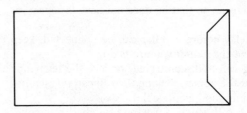

Window – contains a transparent 'window' opening, so the name and address does not need to be typed on the envelope.

Aperture – as above, but with an uncovered address panel.

Suppliers of stationery

Refer to Yellow Pages and the firms listed on p 20 for office forms and stationery.

Telecommunications

Telephone

When answering the telephone:

1 Answer promptly when the telephone rings and state your name or your firm's name.

2 Do not say 'Hello' as this wastes time and does not help the caller.

3 Try not to keep a caller waiting. If there is likely to be a long delay in connecting the caller, it may be better to ring him back and save his time on the telephone. This is particularly important if the call is made from a call-box telephone where the caller may not have the additional coins.

4 Have a message pad and pencil at hand so that you can write down a message.

5 You may have to leave the telephone for a while to make an enquiry or collect some information. If so, let the caller know how long you expect to be and ask if he would prefer you to call him back. Arrange for calls to be answered for you.

6   When an incoming call has to be transferred from one extension to another, convey the caller's name and request to the new extension so that he does not have to repeat his message.

7   If there is a delay before a caller can be connected, keep him informed of the action you are taking.

8   If an incoming call is disconnected, replace the telephone receiver so that the person making the call can re-establish the connection as soon as possible.

9   If you receive a call which is a wrong number, remember that the intrusion is not intentional and that it is probably just as irritating to the caller as it is to you. You need not apologise, but one made by the caller should be accepted politely.

10 Always try to greet people cheerfully, even at the end of the day. If you know a caller's name, do not hesitate to use it when speaking to him.

11 A caller who wishes to speak to someone who is absent should not be kept waiting but asked whether he would like to:
    • speak to someone else
    • be rung back when the person returns
    • ring again later
    • leave a message
    Whatever the answer, the caller's name, firm's name and telephone number should be noted.

When making a telephone call:

1   Check the correct code and number before dialling. If you are in doubt, look it up in the dialling instructions booklet (for the code) and the telephone directory (for the number) and write it down.

2   After dialling the number, allow sufficient time for the call to be connected.

3   If you make a mistake while dialling, replace the receiver for a short while and then start dialling again.

4   When the person answers, say who you are and to whom you wish to speak and their extension number, if you know it.

5   If you are connected to a wrong number, remember to apologise. It may be your fault, or it may be the operator's, but it is certainly never the fault of the person called.

6   If a number cannot be dialled, dial 100 and ask the operator to get it for you, stating the number required and your own telephone number.

7   A telephone call should be planned in exactly the same way as a business letter. Even before dialling the number, you should have any necessary papers at hand. It is also advisable to prepare beforehand a short list of points to be discussed.

When making a telephone call abroad:
1 Check the codes and number and write them down. If you do not know them, call International Directory Enquiries by dialling the number given in your local dialling instruction booklet under Operator Services.
2 If you have International Direct Dialling (IDD), you can dial the call yourself. Dial the four groups of digits in the following order:
international code (010)
country code
area code
subscriber's number
3 If you are not sure whether you have IDD, dial 100 and ask the operator. When IDD is unavailable, the call must be placed with the International Operator (dial the number given in your local dialling instruction booklet under Operator Services).
4 Be prepared to wait up to a minute before you are connected because of the long distance involved.
5 Remember the time differences for each country, and that between March and October British Summer Time is one hour later than GMT (see p 150).
6 Note that the tones used in other countries are usually different from those in the UK.

British Telecom telephone services

Advice of Duration and Charge (ADC)	– finding out cost and length of a call
Alarm calls	– exchange rings you at a requested time
Directory enquiries	– enquiring about a telephone number
Financial Times index and business news	– gives the latest FT Industrial Ordinary Share Index and important items of business news
Fixed-time calls	– calls booked in advance to be connected at a specified time
Freefone	– provides for customers or agents to make calls to a firm without payment
Motoring information service	– information about road conditions
Personal calls	– arrange for a call to be connected only when a specified person is on the line
Telephone credit cards	– provides for calls to be made from any telephone without payment at the time

Temporary transfer of calls	– calls automatically transferred from one number to another
Time service	– provides the correct time
Transferred charge calls	– arrange for a call to be charged to the called subscriber's account
Weather information and forecasts	– provides details of local weather conditions and forecasts

Telephone equipment

Callmakers (card and tape)	– automatic dialling of previously selected and stored numbers
Loudspeaking telephone	– enables user to make and receive calls without holding the handset. Also useful for small conferences as the people present can all hear what is said by the incoming caller and anyone at the conference can reply
Radio paging	– 'bleeper' paging device for contacting people when they are away from their offices
Telephone answering machine	– used for answering the telephone, giving callers a prerecorded announcement and recording their message
Telephone writer	– transmits handwritten messages and sketches to any number of receiving stations; can be connected to a telephone

Switchboards

PMBX – Private Manual Branch Exchange	– telephonist makes all connections between extensions within the organisation as well as the incoming and outgoing calls
PABX – Private Automatic Branch Exchange	– external calls can be dialled direct from extensions and extensions can dial one another
Digital switchboards using a micro-computer	– provides many features including call queuing for busy periods; diverting unanswered calls to another extension; the use of different ringing tones to identify outside calls from internal ones; a memory store for regularly called numbers

Telephone alphabet

When it is necessary to emphasise or identify any letter or word it can be done by using the official Post Office alphabetical code, which is as follows:

A	for Alfred	J	for Jack	S	for Samuel
B	for Benjamin	K	for King	T	for Tommy
C	for Charlie	L	for London	U	for Uncle
D	for David	M	for Mary	V	for Victor
E	for Edward	N	for Nellie	W	for William
F	for Frederick	O	for Oliver	X	for X-Ray
G	for George	P	for Peter	Y	for Yellow
H	for Harry	Q	for Queen	Z	for Zebra
I	for Isaac	R	for Robert		

Emergency calls

For the FIRE, POLICE, AMBULANCE, COASTGUARD, CAVE or MOUNTAIN Rescue Services, dial 999 unless the dial label on your telephone states otherwise. It is important to remember that you are connected first to a Post Office operator, who will then put you through to the required emergency service.

When the operator answers give:
a details of the emergency service required
b your telephone number
   When the emergency service answers give:
a the address where help is needed
b all other information for which you are asked.

Telemessage service

The message is telephoned to the Telegraph Office by dialling 100 and asking for Telemessage Service. A 'telegram-style' written message is then delivered by first-class post next morning.

Greetings telemessage

Designed for messages of congratulations and good wishes; printed on attractively-designed greetings forms.

Telex

Telex is the Post Office teleprinter service which combines the speed of the telephone with the authority of the printed word. What is typed on the sending telex is typed at the same time on the telex at the other end of the line. You can send messages to and receive messages from any other telex subscriber in this country and abroad. If a telex is fitted with a perforator and tape-transmitting attachment, messages can be sent automatically at speeds of up to 70 words a minute. Telex tape-punching units, used for the preparation of telex messages, can be prepared on typewriters, word processors and telex pads (a device which transmits hand-written information).

Facsimile telegraphy

This equipment uses the telephone to transmit, within a few minutes, any form of printed, typed or hand-written matter, drawings, diagrams and photographs from one location to another in this country or abroad. Replicas of documents can be sent any distance with complete accuracy by combining the speed of the telephone with the reproduction facility of the office copier.

A facsimile transceiver

Electronic post

Electronic post is a new service which the Post Office has developed for sending mass mailings by wire to be printed and enveloped in a distant centre for delivery through the post. This service is a combination of computer transmission, laser printing and postal delivery. It is being run initially at two centres, at London and Manchester, and it is open to any firm with a computerised mailing list.

Confravision

Confravision is a Post Office closed-circuit television service which links groups of people in different places for conference purposes. Studios are located in London, Birmingham, Bristol, Glasgow and Manchester. Calls can be booked at a minimum of two hours' notice, subject to availability of studios and circuits.

Datel

Post Office services for digital data transmission over telephone or telegraph lines in the form of punched tape directly to and from computers. An international packet switching service is used for access by UK data terminals to and from computer systems abroad.

Sources of information on telecommunication services

British Telecom Guide (with supplements)
Telephone directories and Yellow Pages
Dialling instruction booklets
Telex directories

Suppliers of communication equipment

Air Call PLC, 176–184 Vauxhall Bridge Road, London SW1V 1DX
EMI Industrial Electronics Ltd, Astronaut House, Hounslow Road, Feltham, Middx TW14 9AD
IBM United Kingdom Ltd, 40 Basinghall Street, London EC2P 2DY
ITT Creed Ltd, Lion Buildings, Crowhurst Road, Hollingbury, Brighton BN1 8AL
3M United Kingdom PLC, 3M House, PO Box 1, Bracknell, Berks RG12 1JU
Plessey Communications & Data Systems Ltd, Beeston, Nottingham NG9 1LA

Televised information services

Quick access to a wide range of information through a television receiver is now available by using the BBC and ITV teletext services or the Post Office viewdata service. The teletext services of Ceefax (BBC) and Oracle (ITV) transmit pages of written data to television sets by means of coded electronic pulses. The Post Office viewdata service, Prestel, uses the telephone network to connect the user's television receiver with the computer supplying pages of data. The page of information required is selected by a remote-controlled push-button handset connected to a specially-adapted domestic television receiver.

These services provide information on such topics as foreign and London stock market reports; share prices; foreign exchange rates; commodity prices; weather maps; train and air services; news headlines; entertainment and sport; food guide; guides to manufacturing and service industries; government information; and reference information of all kinds. The *Prestel Users Guide and Directory* (published by Eastern Counties Newspapers PLC) gives full details of the information providers and services available through Prestel.

Translation and interpreter services

Facilities for arranging translations and the hiring of interpreters may be arranged through the following:

Public libraries

Many of the larger libraries maintain registers of translators who reside in their areas and can usually supply the language and specialist subjects offered.

Chambers of Commerce

Language schools and colleges

The Embassy or High Commission of the country concerned (see pp 52–63)

Travel agents

Department of Trade (Export Services and Promotions Division)
Export House, 50 Ludgate Hill, London EC4M 7HO

Travel arrangements

Road

Reference books and sources of information:
AA or *RAC Handbook*
AA and RAC guides for motoring in Europe
ABC Coach and Bus Guide
National Express Service Guide
Telephone numbers of the employer's garage, mechanic and nearest AA and RAC office
Road maps

Final preparations:
1 Arrange for the appropriate road maps and route plans to be available.
2 Verify the weather conditions in the area in which the employer is travelling.
3 Confirm the booking of hotels.
4 Prepare his itinerary (see example on p 146) and include telephone numbers of hotels, appointments, meetings, etc, and have a clear understanding of the times and places where the employer may be contacted.
5 Collect and hand to the employer all the documents required.
6 Prepare a supply of office stationery so that the employer can write letters, reports, etc, during his travels.
7 Discuss outstanding matters.

Rail

Reference books and sources of information:
British Rail Guides, plus a regular supply of the supplementary issues concerning train times
Telephone numbers of the nearest railway stations

Final preparations:
1 Confirm the time, station, platform of departure of train and the time of arrival at destination.
2 Obtain the ticket for the journey plus one for a reserved seat and/or sleeping berth if applicable.
3 Make arrangements for the employer to be met at his destination.
4 Points 3 to 7 under 'Road'.

Sea

Reference books and sources of information:
ABC Shipping Guide
Current visa, passport, baggage, export licence, health and insurance regulations
Telephone number of the local travel agency office
Telephone number of employer's bank for arranging currency and travellers' cheques, etc

Final preparations:
1 Confirm the name of the quay from which he is leaving.
2 Obtain his tickets.
3 See that the employer has his passport, visa, vaccination certificate and any other documents required.
4 Check that adequate labels have been fixed to his baggage, and prepare labels for the return journey.
5 Obtain foreign currency and travellers' cheques.
6 Make arrangements for him to be met at his destination.
7 Points 3 to 7 under 'Road'.

Air

Reference books and sources of information:
ABC World Airways Guide
Current visa, passport, baggage, export licence, health and insurance regulations
Telephone numbers of the nearest air-line booking office and private charter office
Telephone number of the local travel agency office
Telephone number of the employer's bank for arranging currency, travellers' cheques, etc

Final preparations:
1 Confirm the air terminus from which the employer is leaving, details of the time by which he must be there and the actual take-off time.
2 Obtain his tickets.
3 See that the employer has his passport, visa, vaccination certificate and any other documents required.

4   Check that his baggage does not exceed the maximum weight.
5   Obtain foreign currency and travellers' cheques.
6   Make arrangements for him to be met at the airport or air terminus.
7   Points 3 to 7 under 'Road'.

Key factors in planning business visits abroad

Information Useful information for preparing a business trip abroad can be obtained from the Export Services and Promotions Division of the Department of Trade at Export House, 50 Ludgate Hill, London EC4M 7HU. They publish a series of booklets for different countries entitled 'Hints to Business Men' containing general information about the country, such as areas, population, principal cities and towns, climate, clothing, hours of business; travel information relating to passport, visa and health regulations, currency, customs, travel routes, etc; hotels and restaurants; postal, telephone and telegraphic facilities; economic factors; import and exchange control regulations; government and commercial organisations and methods of doing business.

Passport A current passport is essential for visitors entering a foreign country. Standard British passports are issued for a ten-year period. An application form for a new passport or an extension of an existing one can be obtained from local employment offices, post offices and banks. On completion they should be sent to the regional passport office named on the form. Application must be made at least three weeks before departure. The form has to be countersigned and the photograph certified by a British person in authority, such as a bank manager, justice of the peace or head teacher who has known the applicant personally for at least two years.

Visa A visa is also required for entry to many overseas countries. Travel agents can give you advice on visas and can make arrangements for them to be obtained. Application can also be made direct to the consulate of the country to be visited.

Health regulations Establish, well in advance of the visit, the inoculations and vaccinations required for entering the country concerned and obtain the relevant certificates. The local office of the Department of Health and Social Security will supply a leaflet giving details concerning health protection when travelling abroad.

Money See 'Overseas Travel Facilities' on pp 16–17.

Insurance Insurance cover for personal accident, medical treatment and loss of baggage can be arranged directly with an insurance company or by an agent such as a bank or travel agent.

Tickets The airline tickets should be obtained before the day of departure from a travel agent or direct from an airline booking office. Scheduled flights are the most expensive but can be obtained with very little delay and trouble. Cheaper fares are obtainable in such schemes as the advance passenger excursions (APEX); instant purchase excursions (IPEX); budget fares; group fares and standby. You can obtain further details of these schemes from the travel agent or airline.

Business en route World-wide Business Centres at 110 Strand, London WC2 (01 836 8918) provides a business service on British Airways flights which includes secretarial services, meeting facilities, telephone and telex communications.

```
ITINERARY


Friday 1 January 19--


Depart London (Heathrow) Terminal 2          1015 hrs
        Flight BA191

Arrive Paris (Charles de Gaulle)             1105 hrs


Luncheon engagement with
Monsieur Jacques Thievenot (French Agent)
at Hotel Sofitel, Porte de Versailles        1230 hrs
(Telephone: 1 272 52 05)


Depart Paris (Charles de Gaulle)             1645 hrs


Arrive London (Heathrow)                     1735 hrs
        (A company car will meet you
         at Terminal 2)


Meeting with Sir Ronald Briggs at
140 Langham Place, London W1                 1845 hrs


Dinner at Cumberland Hotel, Marble Arch
with Mrs Jones and Sir Ronald Briggs         2000 hrs


Room reserved at Cumberland Hotel
```

A specimen travel itinerary

Sources of information on travel, see p 74.

Travel information

Passenger train service information

Services from London to:

West Yorkshire, North East ⎱	
East Coast to Scotland ⎰	01 278 2477
East Midlands	
North Wales, North West	
West Midlands	01 387 7070
West Coast to Scotland	
West, South Midlands, South Wales	01 262 6767
Southern England	01 928 5100
East Anglia and Essex	01 283 7171
Services from Birmingham	021 643 2711
Bristol	0272 294255
Glasgow	041 221 3223
Leeds	0532 448133
Liverpool	051 709 9696
Manchester	061 832 8353
Newcastle	0632 26262
Sheffield	0742 26411
Ireland via Holyhead, Stranraer	01 387 7070
Ireland via Fishguard	01 262 6767
Continent, Channel Islands and Ireland	01 834 2345
Continent via Hook of Holland	01 247 9812

British Rail phone numbers

Motorail (car carrying) services	01 603 4555
Car-ferry services	01 834 2345
Sleepers	
Euston	01 387 9400
King's Cross	01 837 4200
Paddington	01 723 7000
British Transport hotel reservations	
Central Reservation Service	01 278 4211

British airlines

British Air Ferries Ltd:

Municipal Airport, Southend-on-Sea, Essex	0702 48601

British Airways:

Victoria Terminal, Buckingham Palace Road, London SW1 9SR	01 834 2323
West London Terminal, Cromwell Road, London SW7 4ED	01 370 4255
Speedbird House, London Airport, Heathrow, Middlesex	01 759 5511
All reservations	01 370 5411
Flight enquiries, Heathrow	01 759 2525

British Caledonian Airways:

215 Piccadilly, London W1V 0AD	01 668 4222

British Midland Airways:

East Midlands Airport, Castle Donington, Nr. Derby DE7 2SB	0332 810552

Loganair Ltd:

Glasgow Airport, Abbotsinch, Paisley PA3 2TG	041 889 3181

Passenger Immunisation and Medical Centres

Victoria Terminal	01 834 2323
Heathrow Airport	01 759 5511

Airport phone numbers

Aberdeen	0224 722331
Alderney	048 182 2888
Belfast	0232 29271
Birmingham	021 743 4272
Bournemouth (Northbourne)	020 16 71177
Bristol (Lulsgate)	027 587 4441
Cardiff (Rhoose)	0446 710296
Carlisle	0228 73641
Cork, Eire (ask first for Irish Republic)	021 965388
Coventry	0203 301717
Dublin, Eire	0001 379900
East Midlands (Derby)	0332 810621
Edinburgh	031 333 1000
Exeter	0392 67433
Glasgow	041 887 1111
Guernsey	0481 37766
Inverness	0463 32471
Islay (Port Ellen)	0496 2361
Isle of Man (Castletown)	062 482 3311
Jersey	0534 41272
Kirkwall, Orkney	0856 2421

Leeds, Bradford (Rawdon)	0532 503431
Liverpool	051 427 4101
London, Gatwick (Crawley)	0293 28822
London, Heathrow	01 759 4321
Luton	0582 36061
Lydd	0679 20401
Manchester	061 437 5233
Newcastle	0632 860966
Newquay (St Mawgan)	063 74 270
Norwich	0603 44288
Plymouth	0752 772752
Prestwick	0292 79822
Shannon, Eire (ask first for Irish Republic)	061 61666
Southampton	0703 612341
Southend-on-Sea	0702 40201
Stansted (Bishop's Stortford)	0279 502387
Stornoway	0851 2256
Sumburgh, Shetland	0950 60654
Teesside (Dinsdale)	0325 332811
Wick	0955 2215

Airline addresses

Aer Lingus – Irish:	
223 Regent Street, London W1	01 734 1212
(Transatlantic)	01 437 8000
Aeroflot Ltd, Soviet Airlines:	
69–72 Piccadilly, London W1V 9HH	01 493 7436
Air Canada:	
140–144 Regent Street, London W1R 6AT	01 439 7941
Air France:	
158 New Bond Street, London W1Y 0AY	
Reservations	01 499 9511
Other enquiries	01 499 8611
Alitalia Italian Airlines:	
251 Regent Street, London W1R 8AQ	01 734 4040
El Al Israel Airlines Ltd:	
185 Regent Street, London W1R 8BS	01 437 9255
Iberia International Airlines of Spain:	
169 Regent Street, London W1R 8BE	
European reservations	01 437 5622
Intercontinental reservations	01 439 7539
Icelandair:	
73 Grosvenor Street, London W1X 9DD	01 499 9971
Japan Air Lines Co Ltd:	
8 Hanover Street, London W1R 0DR	01 408 1000

KLM Royal Dutch Airlines:
    Time & Life Building, 153 New Bond Street
    London W1Y 0AD   01 568 9144
Lufthansa German Airlines:
    23–28 Piccadilly, London W1V 0EJ   01 408 0442
Olympic Airways – Greek:
    141 New Bond Street, London W1Y 0BB   01 493 7262
Pakistan International Airlines:
    45–46 Picadilly, London W1V 0LD   01 439 4200
Pan American World Airways Inc:
    193 Piccadilly, London W1V 0AD   01 409 0688
Qantas Airways Ltd:
    49 Old Bond Street, London W1X 4AQ   01 995 1344
    Ticket Sales Office   01 995 1361
Sabena Belgian World Airlines:
    36 Piccadilly, London W1V 0BU   01 437 6950
SAS Scandinavian Airlines:
    52 Conduit Street, London W1R 0AY   01 734 4020
South African Airways:
    251–259 Regent Street, London W1R 7AD   01 734 9841
Swissair:
    3 New Coventry Street, London W1V 4BJ   01 439 4144
Trans World Airlines Inc:
    200 Piccadilly, London W1   01 636 4090

Time differences

The map below gives a general idea of the time differences
throughout the world in relation to Greenwich Mean Time.
Note that between March and October British Summer Time is
one hour later than GMT.

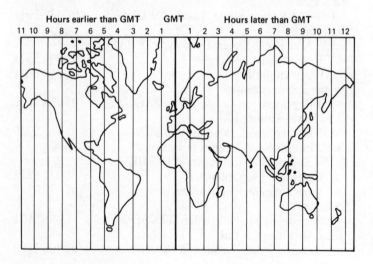

Underground travel in London

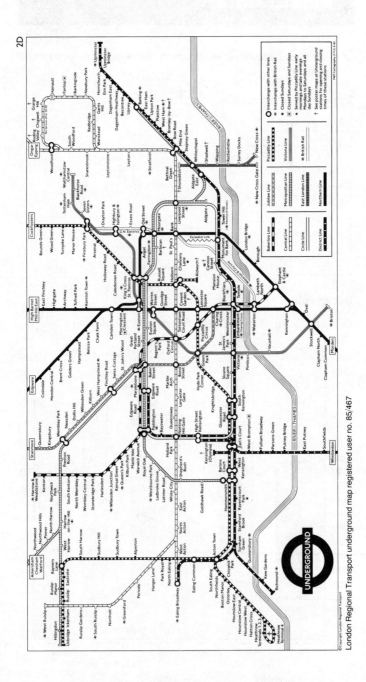

London Regional Transport underground map registered user no. 85/467

Visual data

The following are some of the methods of presenting information visually.

Typewritten tabulation

SALES FOR JANUARY TO JUNE 19--

Month	Home	Export	Total
	£	£	£
January	2000	2500	4500
February	3500	3000	6500
March	4250	2750	7000
April	4000	3250	7250
May	4500	4000	8500
June	3000	4250	7250
Totals	21250	19750	41000

Bar graph

(Showing same data as in the typewritten tabulation)

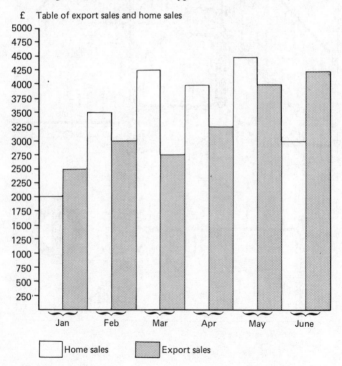

Table of export sales and home sales

☐ Home sales   ▨ Export sales

Line graph

(Showing same data as in typewritten tabulation)

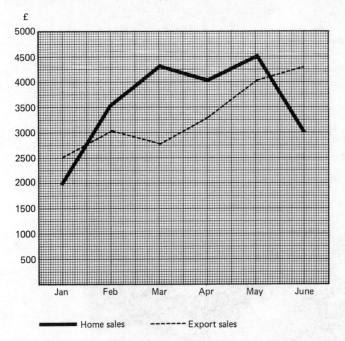

Home sales ------- Export sales

Pie chart

(Using figures for June extracted from typewritten tabulation)

Export sales and home sales for June 19---

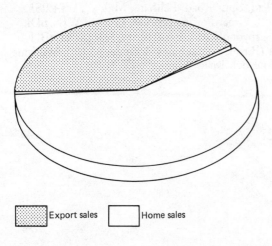

Export sales   Home sales

Visual control board

Suppliers of visual control boards

Carter–Parratt (VISI Record) Ltd, Visi Record House, 38 Kimpton Road, Sutton, Surrey SM3 3QD
Esselte Dymo Ltd, Spur Road, Feltham, Middx TW14 0SL
Ryman Ltd, 6–10 Great Portland Street, London W1N 6DL
Sasco Ltd, 36 Croydon Road, Beckenham, Kent BR3 4BH
Peter Williams (Business Machines & Systems) Ltd, Williams House, 821 Woolwich Road, London SE7 8LS

Weights and measures

Imperial measures and equivalents   *Metric measures and equivalents*

Length

1 inch	= 12 inches	= 2.5400 cm	1 centimetre (cm)	= 10 millimetres	= 0.3937 in
1 foot	= 3 feet	= 0.3048 m	1 metre (m)	= 100 cm	= 1.0936 yd
1 yard	= 5.5 yards	= 0.9144 m	1 kilometre (km)	= 1000 m	= 0.6214 mile
1 rod	= 22 yards	= 5.0292 m			
1 chain	= 220 yards	= 20.117 m			
1 furlong	= 1760 yards	= 201.17 m			
1 mile	= 6080 feet	= 1.6093 km			
1 nautical mile		= 1.8532 km			

Surface or area

1 sq in	= 144 sq inches	= 6.4516 cm^2	1 sq cm (cm^2)	= 100 mm^2	= 0.1550 sq in
1 sq ft	= 9 sq feet	= 0.0929 m^2	1 sq metre (m^2)	= 10 000 cm^2	= 1.1960 sq yd
1 sq yd	= 4840 sq yards	= 0.8361 m^2	1 are (a)	= 100 m^2	= 119.60 sq yd
1 acre	= 640 acres	= 4046.86 m^2	1 hectare (ha)	= 100 ares	= 2.4711 acres
1 sq mile		= 259.0 hectares	1 sq km (km^2)	= 100 hectares	= 0.3861 sq miles

Imperial measures and equivalents

Capacity

1 cu inch		= 16.387 cm³
1 cu foot	= 1728 cu inches	= 0.0283 m³
1 cu yard	= 27 cu feet	= 0.7646 m³
1 pint	= 4 gills	= 0.5683 litres
1 quart	= 2 pints	= 1.1365 litres
1 gallon	= 8 pints	= 4.5461 litres
1 bushel	= 8 gallons	= 36.369 litres

Weight

1 ounce (oz)	= 437½ grains	= 28.350 gm
1 pound (lb)	= 16 ounces	= 0.4536 kg
1 stone	= 14 pounds	= 6.3503 kg
1 hundredweight (cwt)	= 112 pounds	= 50.802 kg
1 ton	= 20 cwt	= 1.0161 tonnes

Metric measures and equivalents

1 cu cm (cm³)		= 0.0610 cu in
1 cu metre (m³)	= 999.972 litres	= 1.3080 cu yd
1 litre (l)	= 1.000028 dm³	= 1.7598 pints
1 hectolitre (hl)	= 100 litres	= 2.7497 bushels

1 milligram (mg)		= 0.0154 grain
1 gram (g)	= 1000 mg	= 0.0353 oz
1 kilogram (kg)	= 1000 g	= 2.2046 lb
1 quintal (q)	= 100 kg	= 1.9684 cwt
1 tonne (t)	= 10 q	= 0.9842 ton

Personal reminders

Name

Address

Postal code

Telephone

Business address

Telephone

Car registration no

Car key nos											
Car licence due											
Driving licence no											
Credit card no											
Passport no											
TV licence due											
Blood group											
National insurance no.											
Notes:											

Telephone index of numbers used frequently

Name	Organisation	Telephone	
		Code	Number

Local government authorities

County council	Name	Address	Telephone no	Department	Name of contact
Planning					
Highways					
Police					
Fire Service					
Consumer protection					
Recreation					
Museums					
Education*					
Social services*					
Libraries*					

*Non-metropolitan County and Metropolitan District Councils

District council	Name	Address	Telephone no	Department	Name of contact
Local planning					
Housing					
Highways					
Building regulations					
Environmental health					
Refuse collection					
Cemeteries					
Recreation					
Museums					
Parish council Allotments					
Community halls					
Recreation					
Cemeteries					

Local offices of government departments

	Address	Telephone no	Name of contact
Customs and Excise			
Health and Social Security			
Electricity Board			
Gas Board			
Inland Revenue			
Manpower Services Commission			
Employment Services Division (Job Centre)			
Training Services Division			
Post Office			
Railway			
Training Board			

Index